IMAGES OF
CANADA
A Nation in Postage Stamps

IMAGES OF CANADA

A Nation in Postage Stamps

GORDON DONALDSON

Foreword by
PIERRE BERTON

Éditions Grosvenor Inc.
Montréal - Toronto

Publication of this book was made possible through the sponsorship of the Canada Post Corporation.

Copyright © 1990, Grosvenor House Press, Inc.

All rights reserved.

No part of this publication may be reproduced or transmitted in any form or by any means, electronic or mechanical, including photocopy, recording, or any information storage and retrieval system now known or to be invented, without permission in writing from the publisher, except by a reviewer who wishes to quote brief passages in connection with a review written for inclusion in a magazine, newspaper, or broadcast.

Canadian Cataloguing in Publication Data

Donaldson, Gordon, 1926 -
Images of Canada: a nation in postage stamps

Issued also in French under title:
Images du Canada : l'histoire par le timbre-poste

ISBN 0-919959-57-1

1. Postage-stamps — Canada.   2. Postage-stamps — Topics-Canada — History.   3. Canada — History — Miscellanea. I. Title.

HE6185.C2D66 1990   769.56'3'0971   C90-090480-1

Published by

Grosvenor House Press Inc.
99 Queen Street East
Suite 302
Toronto, Ontario
M5C 1S1

Éditions Grosvenor Inc.
1456, rue Sherbrooke ouest
Montréal, Québec
H3G 1K4

Edited by Joan Irving
Cover design by William D. Marler
Printed and bound in Canada

Stamps reproduced with the permission of the Canada Post Corporation and the Canadian Postal Archives.

Contents

Foreword		7
Introduction		9
1	The Explorers	11
2	The Settlers	19
3	The Leaders	27
4	Kings and Queens	35
5	Pioneering Women	65
6	The Environment	71
7	First Peoples	75
8	Transportation and Communication	79
9	Industry and War	87
10	Sporting Stamps	91

Foreword

In 1904 the young Prince of Wales, heir apparent to the throne of England, received a telephone call from his equerry, Sir Arthur Davidson. "Did you happen to see in the papers that some damned fool has given as much as fourteen hundred pounds for one stamp?" Davidson asked. Back came the restrained tones of the future George V: "I was that damned fool."

What is it that drives kings and cobblers to search out postage stamps both rare and commonplace, sometimes to the exclusion of any other leisure activity? George V's collection absorbed him for the last 30 years of his life. Come war or crisis, he spent three afternoons a week in his stamp room, giving himself over so completely to these sessions that his aides could remember only two occasions when he interrupted his activities to ring for a servant.

If stamp collecting is an obsession, it is an honorable and a rewarding one. Consider the Canadian schoolboy who collects his country's stamps. He gives himself, no doubt unwittingly, a thorough course in his nation's geography and history, in its triumphs and tragedies, in its heroes and villains. The whole drama of the Canadian experience, from the opening of the frontier to the victories and defeats in war, is there for him to contemplate.

Even in the jet age it is difficult for anyone to gain a complete sense of country. Our population islands, separated by vast barriers, are strung out like beads on a string along a 7,000-kilometre strip that is only about 300 kilometres wide. The rest is largely rock and muskeg, forest and tundra, mountains, lake and river. But anybody can visit this hinterland vicariously through the tiny, exquisite illustrations in the stamp album.

1969 Vincent Massey

Those who collect Canadian stamps will never say our history has been dull. From Samuel Hearne to Molly Brant, from Louis Riel to Josiah Henson, from Paul Kane to Vincent Massey, the men and women who helped create Canadian history have been commemorated on the stamps of the nation. How satisfying it is to contemplate that the great milestones of the past—from the discovery of "newe founde lande" to Expo 67—have all been recorded in miniature.

1971 Paul Kane, painter

Think of the Niagara of correspondence that surges daily along that 7,000-kilometre strip — business letters and love letters, dunning letters and greeting cards, birth notices and gossip, angry letters, passionate letters, pleading letters, boring letters and letters edged in black. Many carry a second message on the envelope's upper-right corner in the form of a tiny picture that fits neatly into the jigsaw puzzle of people, events and natural splendor that delineates Canada's heritage.

A stamp, of course, is a form of receipt, and a very visible one, but it is more than that. It reminds us of who we are. It takes us back to our beginnings. And it tells us that, whatever our faults and strengths, we are and always have been unique.

Pierre Berton

Introduction

In 1840 Britain issued the Penny Black, the world's first adhesive postage stamp. Canada added interest and beauty to stamps in 1851, when it issued one of the world's first pictorial stamps — the Threepence Beaver.

It was designed by Sir Sandford Fleming, an exuberant Scots-born engineer who recognized that stamps were more than a means of improving mail service: they had enduring historical and artistic value. Fleming's picture of a beaver was a tribute not only to the animal and its fur — for beaver pelts had been a source of wealth for the early colonists — but confirmation of a Canadian postal system. In 1850 the three colonial governments of Canada (Ontario and Québec), New Brunswick and Nova Scotia had won the right to set up their own postal systems. Then came Fleming's Threepence Beaver, the first "Canada Postage" stamp.

1851 Threepence Beaver

1977 Sir Sandford Fleming, designer of Canada's first stamp.

Mail is as old as recorded history. A postal service began in Egypt around 2,000 BC and in China about one thousand years later. The earliest surviving letters are baked clay tablets in clay envelopes, delivered in Asia Minor about 3,000 BC.

The Romans used special chariots to haul mail across their empire. A postal guide listing Roman relay stations still exists, engraved on silver goblets known as the Apollinaire vases.

Canada's first general postal service was established in 1763 by Benjamin Franklin, then Joint Deputy Postmaster General of British North America. He arranged for riders to carry the mail, for six cents a league (three miles), between Montréal, Trois-Rivières and Québec City. Franklin's contribution to the Canadian postal system was commemorated in 1976, the bicentennial of the United States.

1976 Benjamin Franklin, who established Canada's first general postal service.

Before the advent of postage stamps, the recipient had to pay a fee when a letter was delivered — if he wanted it. Often he would glance at the envelope and hand it back, saying he couldn't afford the high postal rates: The writer had inserted prearranged code words in the address so that the message got across free.

In 1834 Toronto had one postman to serve its 9,000 inhabitants, and he demanded a penny a letter for delivery. Sixteen years later the city still had only one postman, but he was now serving 21,000 people and demanding two cents a letter.

1987 First Toronto Post Office

The adhesive stamp, meant to ensure that letters were prepaid by the sender, was introduced in Great Britain in 1840 by Sir Rowland Hill. The Penny Black, as it was known, bore a portrait of the young Queen Victoria. The United States adopted the adhesive stamp in 1847, four years ahead of the colonies in British North America. During that interval, letters from Canada to the U.S. had to be prepaid in cash as far as the border, then carry American stamps to pay the fee for the rest of the distance.

Canada, New Brunswick and Nova Scotia produced their own stamps until Confederation, in 1867, when the Dominion Post Office Department was created in Ottawa. British Columbia, Prince Edward Island and Newfoundland continued to issue their own stamps until each joined Confederation, in 1871, 1873 and 1949, respectively.

Despite the growing use of stamps, some people preferred the old method of sending unstamped letters and letting the recipient pay. But the practice began to die out after 1875, when the Postmaster General ordered that all mail without stamps go straight to the Dead Letter Office. A special stamp for the Dead Letter Office was issued between 1879 and 1913. It presents a gloomy picture of Queen Victoria with the information that the undeliverable letter had been opened to trace the whereabouts of the sender, then resealed and mailed back from the postal grave.

In the big cities, letter carriers were given tickets to travel by horse-drawn streetcar. By the turn of the century, they were supplied with four-wheeled bikes and electric Royal Mail trucks. Special trains carrying a sorting office began running between Montréal and Toronto in 1854. The sorters, who worked by night in swaying cars, were the elite of the postal service.

1980 Curtiss JN-4 *Canuck*, used for first airmail flight from Montréal to Toronto in 1918.

The first official flight to carry mail was from Montréal to Toronto, by biplane in 1918. Regular airmail service did not begin until 10 years later.

Organized philately began in Canada in 1887, although stamp collectors had been at work since May, 1840, when Dr. John Edward Gray, of the British Museum, bought a block of Penny Blacks. This and other issues he had collected were listed in his 1863 stamp catalogue, one of the first of its kind.

Canada's most famous and most beautiful stamps — in fact examples of every stamp issued after 1851 — are preserved in Ottawa, at the National Archives.

Over the years, hundreds of stamps have been issued to commemorate the nation's great men and women, its unparalleled natural resources, the birds and animals that are found here — and some that are close to extinction — and the machines that have helped Canadians to open up this vast nation. It would be impossible to discuss each stamp, but in the following pages we present you with a selection of people and events from Canada's past, as reflected in postage stamps.

Chapter One

The Explorers

A sudden wind cleared the fog as the stubby little ship *Matthew* wallowed in unknown waters. The night sky grew bright, for it was June 24, and in those northern latitudes it is never completely dark in midsummer. Master mariner John Cabot could smell land ahead, and at 5 a.m. he sighted it — "the newe founde lande."

He sailed cautiously toward it, taking soundings, and found an anchorage, probably in Griquet Harbour on the island's northern tip. There he landed, formed a procession behind a ship's boy carrying a crozier, and took possession of Newfoundland in the name of Henry VII of England. He planted the flags of St. George for the king and St. Mark of Venice for himself because Cabot, or Caboto, was Venetian.

1949 Newfoundland issue marking that province's entry into Confederation. It shows Cabot's ship, the *Matthew*.

His landing, in 1497, established Britain's claim on the New World and marked the beginning of recorded Canadian history.

Cabot would have been surprised to find himself honored, 402 years later, on a Canadian stamp, for he thought he had reached Asia. He remains a mystery man. His origins, his name and his eventual fate are unknown. There are no portraits of him, so the 1949 Canadian stamp shows his ship. In 1897 Newfoundland issued a "John Cabot" stamp but used a portrait of his son, Sebastian. John Cabot left no sea journal or letters, not even a signature. All we know is that King Henry paid Cabot 10 pounds for finding him his first colony, the foundation of the British Empire. Cabot is said to have spent it on flashy clothes, while his son Sebastian claimed credit for the voyage.

He sailed again in 1498, but his ship disappeared and the explorer was presumed lost at sea.

Soon after Cabot, French, English and Portuguese crews began fishing regularly on the Newfoundland banks. One crew was led by the Breton captain Jacques Cartier. By now it was recognized that Newfoundland was not Asia but possibly the key to Asia; somewhere along its shores, or to the north or south, lay the fabled Northwest Passage, gateway to the mysterious East.

1897 Newfoundland Cabot

1934 Cartier Commemorative

1984 Cartier and ship

1908 Cartier and Champlain

In 1534 Cartier was commissioned by the King of France, François I, to lead an expedition through the Strait of Belle Isle, north of Newfoundland, in search of the passage and any precious metals he might find along the way. France, like England, was jealous of the golden treasure that Spain was digging out of the Americas and wanted a share.

Cartier took one look at the dark seas and bleak rocks of Labrador, called it "the land God gave Cain," and sailed south for the Gulf of St. Lawrence, past Prince Edward Island and into the Baie de Gaspé. Here the sun shone, the forests shimmered and the dolphins gambolled cheerfully around his ship. "The climate is more temperate than Spain," Cartier reported, "the soil the fairest you could see anywhere, and the waters are teeming with salmon."

A 400th anniversary stamp shows Cartier raising a cross to claim for France the land and the great waterway that he thought was the Northwest Passage.

He sailed home, to return in 1535 with an ambitious three-ship expedition. He named the bay of St. Laurent after the popular Breton saint (the name later extended to the gulf and river) and pushed on as far as the narrows below Cape Diamond, the great rock of Québec. Here would be located Québec City, cradle of New France in America.

In the Iroquois language, "kebec" means narrowing-place, and the Iroquois village he landed at, called Stadacona, was a "kanata," or settlement. Thus the future province and nation got their names. Farther upstream Cartier reached another village, Hochelaga, beneath a peak which he named Mont Royale. He could sail no farther; above this point were shallow rapids. The Kingdom of Saguenay, rich in gold, silver and copper, lay beyond and out of reach. The rapids that barred the seaway to the interior, quashing hopes that the St. Lawrence was the passage to the Far East, were named, sardonically, Lachine (China).

Cartier spent the winter in Hochelaga, planning to climb the rapids the following spring, but cold and scurvy decimated his crews and instead he returned home to find France at war and further exploration postponed for the duration.

Cartier's attempts to establish a colony on the St. Lawrence failed mainly because the gold dust shipped back to France turned out to be fool's gold. The French coined a new saying, "not worth a Canadian diamond," and New France was officially ignored for 60 years.

Cartier shares a stamp with the later, successful colonizer Samuel de Champlain, who arrived in New France in 1608.

Meanwhile, the English were probing to the north where the Northwest Passage actually was, though they didn't find it. In fact, the first successful navigation had to wait until this century, by which time the magic waterway was useless for commerce. But the voyages of Martin Frobisher, John Davis, Henry Hudson and

William Baffin mapped a huge, hitherto unknown area of Canada and left the explorers' names on immense bays and straits.

Frobisher, a dour Yorkshireman, was one of Queen Elizabeth's beloved seadogs; an adventurer, privateer and sometime jailbird, the mighty man whose portrait appears on a 1963 stamp was not to be trifled with. On his first expedition, in 1576, he sailed his *Gabriel* up Frobisher Strait, as he called it, proclaiming it to be "the Passage to Cathay," dividing America and Asia. After 150 miles he came to a dead end. This was not a passage but a bay, so it became Frobisher Bay.

1963 Martin Frobisher, who helped to map Canada's northern coasts.

The next year he was back, with three ships and the title "High Admiral of all seas and waters, countries, lands and isles as well as of Cathay." While becalmed off Greenland his men caught a "hollibut" big enough to feed the entire ship's company and make some of them sick from overeating. Dodging icebergs, they sailed back into Frobisher Bay and landed. They battled with the Inuit — their loaded firearms, arquebuses, against bows and arrows — but failed to free the five sailors the Inuit had captured the year before. They returned to England with gifts for the queen — a narwhal tusk and three cargoes of "gold ore" that initial assays indicated was valuable.

On the third voyage Frobisher lost his way and blundered into what would become Hudson Strait. Though he nearly lost his fleet to do so, he brought back more ore. But attempts to smelt precious metal out of it failed, and the entire three-year collection ended up being used to repair holes in English roads.

1987

Étienne Brûlé, described as "an immortal scoundrel," was the first European to see Niagara Falls and lakes Ontario, Huron and Superior. He camped at the site of present-day Toronto.

He came to Québec from France in 1608 as a 16-year-old servant in Champlain's household but soon took to the woods, where he lived with the Hurons, learning their language. Champlain frowned upon the wild young man's ways but used him as an interpreter and liaison officer. This permitted Brûlé to roam at will without being outlawed.

Étienne explored more for fun than for profit or glory. He never wrote his great adventure story because he couldn't write, but few travellers covered as much of the country.

1983 Sir Humphrey Gilbert, who claimed Newfoundland for England.

Frobisher was a great seaman but a poor prospector. His associate and successor, Sir Humphrey Gilbert, was no sailor but he had advanced, liberal ideas on how to run a colony. Sent by the queen in 1583 to colonize Newfoundland, Gilbert claimed it for England (although Cabot had already done so). But he had landed in August, too late to build a colony before winter, and so he set sail for home. During the voyage his small frigate *Squirrel* encountered a fierce storm. St. Elmo's fire, the sailors' omen of disaster, flamed along the yardarm. Captain Edward Hayes of the *Golden Hind* brought his larger ship alongside and begged Gilbert to come aboard. According to Hayes, Gilbert shouted "We are as neare to heaven by sea as by land." At the time Gilbert had been reading Sir Thomas More's *Utopia*, which contains the passage: "The way to heaven out of all places is of like length and distance." That night Hayes watched the *Squirrel*'s lights suddenly go out as it was "devoured and swallowed up of the sea." Gilbert, the Utopian, was ahead of his time. The colonization of Canada lay in the future.

While the British probed Canada's mysteries by ship, the French were reaching out across the continent over land, lake and stream. The bark canoe they had adopted from the natives took them where no sea vessel could go, faster than on horseback and, despite the back-breaking portages, easier than on foot. The great French explorers were a unique breed of men; iron-hard and stubborn, yet restless as quicksilver, they were driven ever farther into the cruel wilderness by the urge to find and claim new lands. They had no interest in settling. Their strong faces, depicted on stamps, indicate their stalwart characters.

One of the greatest of these was René-Robert Cavelier, Sieur de La Salle. He was arrogant, as befitted his noble birth, dedicated as a result of his years in a Jesuit novitiate and impatient to make a fortune because he was hounded by creditors. In 1677 he conceived the grandiose plan of seizing the entire West of the continent, from Niagara Falls extending as far as the imagination could reach. He would build a line of fortified fur-trade posts out to the Upper Lakes and down the Ohio Valley to the mighty Mississippi, which he believed led to the western sea. This would pen the English, Dutch and Spanish colonists into enclaves along the eastern seaboard and leave the great interior to France — and to La Salle, who had received exclusive trading rights from the king.

1966 Cavelier de La Salle, one of the first Europeans to venture into Canada's West.

In 1679 he travelled to Niagara Falls. He was one of the first white men to see the falls. He built both a fort and a ship, the *Griffon*, which was to be the first vessel larger than a canoe to sail the Upper Lakes. The ship, along with La Salle and his navigational tools and maps, is depicted in a 1966 stamp. While construction was going on, he commuted on snowshoes to Fort Frontenac (now Kingston, Ontario) and Montréal to raise more money and put off his creditors. Despite his goodwill these trips seldom ended pleasantly. At one dinner party in Montréal, he was offered salad laced with hemlock, and at another the wine turned cloudy because it had been spiked with arsenic.

La Salle survived to sail the *Griffon* as far as Green Bay, Wisconsin, where he met a trading party with enough beaver and buffalo skins to keep his grand scheme alive. He loaded the cargo onto his ship and ordered it back to Niagara. En route, the *Griffon* vanished — either sunk in a storm, attacked by Indians or scuttled by its crew who made off with the furs. Nobody knows for sure.

La Salle built a new fort and shipyard, Fort Broken Heart, on the Illinois River and returned to Niagara to find his stronghold there in ashes. He soon received word that Fort Broken Heart had also been burned and that a ship bringing him supplies from France had been wrecked in the St. Lawrence.

Yet, on April 9, 1682, he would stand on the shore of his "western sea," actually the Gulf of Mexico, erect a wooden cross and claim for France "possession of this country of Louisiana." His Louisiana stretched all the way back up the Mississippi to the Ohio. But La Salle was no colonizer. Five years later, when he returned to settle his great empire, his men mutinied and murdered him, and La Salle was left to the buzzards in a Texas swamp.

Although La Salle had claimed a third of the continent, two ragged rascals in a canoe played an equally important role in its exploration. Pierre-Esprit Radisson and his brother-in-law Médard Chouart, Sieur des Groseilliers, opened the fur treasury of the great northwest and became the founders of the Hudson's Bay Company, owned by the British.

1987 Radisson and des Groseilliers, *coureurs de bois*

"We were Caesars, [there] being nobody to contradict us," Radisson wrote. The Caesars were swindled by both the British and French authorities — which made them switch allegiances frequently — but they survived.

The two adventurers began as *coureurs de bois*, or woodrunners, the unlicensed fur traders of New France who roved and hunted with the natives in the exhilarating freedom of the wilds. The two traders reached Lake Superior in 1659, then paddled north to the fringes of Hudson Bay, and returned with an impressive load of furs and tales of the huge profits to be made there. The governor, inspired by greed and the Jesuits' war on the *coureurs*, jailed Radisson and Groseilliers and confiscated their cargo.

The partners later took their story to King Charles II, in London, who helped them raise money for an exploratory voyage to be taken along Henry Hudson's route into his bay. Sailing on Hudson's famous ship the *Nonsuch*, which has a stamp of its own, Groseilliers brought back furs worth 19,000 pounds — enough to convince the king to charter the Governor and Company of Adventurers of England, Trading into Hudson's Bay (1670). It was to become one of the world's most profitable businesses, but Radisson and Groseilliers got little more than a gold chain and medal apiece for their great pioneering efforts.

1968 *Nonsuch*, Henry Hudson's ship

1958 de la Verendrye

1978 Captain Cook

1978 Nootka Sound, Cook's landfall on Canada's west coast.

1988 George Vancouver

They turned to France and helped found the Compagnie du Nord, which was soon challenging the British Lords of the North. Radisson captured a British fur ship and became a popular hero in Québec. But the new governor fined him and shipped him back to France, while Groseilliers retired to his gooseberry fields at Trois-Rivières. Radisson turned his coat once again and rejoined the Hudson's Bay Company, this time as a shareholder. He led profitable fur-trading voyages until he died in London at the age of 76.

In 1731 a French army officer, Pierre de Varennes, Sieur de la Verendrye, pushed farther west than had any explorer before him. He built forts at Lake of the Woods, Lake Winnipeg and the Assiniboine River, then moved on to the upper Missouri and the Black Hills region, thus opening up the Dakotas, western Minnesota and Manitoba.

Toward the end of the French regime (1759), the supermen-explorers of New France were dying out. Yet only about half of Canada had been explored. The torch was seized again by the British, who began probing the west coast. Since no one had been able to find the Northwest Passage from the east, the British Admiralty decided to look for its western end. In 1776 they assigned their greatest navigator, Captain James Cook, to the task. Cook, 48, had risen from the lower decks to a navy captain's cabin, an unusual feat for a man of humble origins. He had been a ship's master, or chief petty officer, on General James Wolfe's seaborne invasion of Québec and gone on to sail twice around the world, take possession of Australia and chart that continent's coastline as well as those of New Guinea, New Zealand, various South Sea islands and parts of the Antarctic.

He had, in short, been everywhere. Along the way he had conquered fever and scurvy at sea by making his men eat sauerkraut and grain malt, which provided the vitamin C necessary to their diets.

On this two-year voyage, his last, Cook took the sloops *Resolution* and *Discovery* round the southern tip of Africa, across the Indian Ocean and into the Pacific, stopped to discover the Hawaiian islands and made landfall on the Canadian west coast at Nootka Sound. His orders were to sail north as far as he could, looking into every inlet for the elusive passage. Thus he sailed up to and through the Bering Strait, charting the entire coastline as he progressed. (Before Cook, the only maps of this coast were Russian and so wildly inaccurate that they depicted Alaska as an island.) At the strait Cook was blocked by a wall of ice and he turned back, without finding the passage. He revisited Hawaii and was killed there in a scuffle with natives over a stolen boat.

George Vancouver, a midshipman on Cook's last voyage, commanded an expedition to Nootka Sound three years later. He circumnavigated the island he had first visited with Cook, giving it (and the city on the mainland) his name.

Captain Cook had established that major northern rivers did not empty into the Pacific. So where did their water go? Alexander Mackenzie, a 25-year-old Scot who was a partner in the North West Company, believed there must be a large river still undiscovered. In 1789 he left Fort Chipewyan, in present-day Alberta, with some Indian guides and a crew of French-Canadian voyageurs in four large canoes. Six days' paddling brought them down the Great Slave River to Great Slave Lake. There the guides learned that there was an even greater river at the lake's western end and, after another four days' paddling, Mackenzie and his crew arrived at what is now the Mackenzie River. They continued their journey, covering up to 100 miles a day through swarms of mosquitoes, until they reached the mouth of the river, on the Arctic Ocean. It was here, on a later expedition, that Mackenzie painted on a stone the famous inscription, which also appears on his commemorative stamp, "Alex Mackenzie, from Canada by land, 22nd July 1793."

1970 Alexander Mackenzie, who led an expedition to the mouth of the river named for him, on the Arctic Ocean.

1971

Samuel Hearne was described as the Marco Polo of the Barren Lands. Between 1770 and 1772 he explored a vast area of Canada's northland, covering many thousands of miles on foot.

Hearne started as a midshipman in the Royal Navy, was hired as a seaman by the Hudson's Bay Company and was stationed at Fort Prince of Wales (Churchill, Manitoba). From there, the company sent him northward to explore the Copper Mine River and see if he could find the Northwest Passage along the way. He reached the mouth of the Copper Mine River on his third attempt. What was more important, he learned how to survive in the Barren Lands and wrote an account of the region and its animals that would become a bible for future explorers.

1988 Simon Fraser

Simon Fraser followed, to name his river and later open trading posts along the upper Peace River. David Thompson spent 27 years travelling by foot, horseback and canoe to chart almost two million square miles of wilderness and produce the first comprehensive map of western Canada.

There was much exploring yet to be done, but the general extent and nature of Canada was now known. The next step was to settle the land and fill some of the hard-won territory with people.

1957 David Thompson

Chapter Two

The Settlers

*I*n 1608 Samuel de Champlain founded Québecq (an early spelling), the first permanent French settlement in Canada. Three hundred years later a series of stamps, Canada's first bilingual postage stamps, was issued in commemoration of this event.

Champlain and his men built a trading post on the shores of the St. Lawrence, below the grey cliffs that rose to the prow-shaped pinnacle of Cape Diamond. It had stout log walls and was surrounded by a ditch. From that small foothold Champlain, a sailor's son and royal geographer, planned to develop the entire continent.

He founded Québec with 32 people. More arrived the next spring when the ice broke and ships could enter the river, but the adventurous young men were more interested in living and hunting with the natives than in the back-breaking work of starting farms. Many became *coureurs de bois* and worked in the fur trade with the friendly Huron and Montagnais peoples who lived along the St. Lawrence.

1958 Samuel de Champlain, founder of Québec, the first permanent French settlement in Canada.

To the southwest lay the Iroquois territory of the League of the Five Nations, the most powerful empire on the continent. It had been guided by its own democratic principles and it had been master of northern New York since the legendary Hiawatha.

In 1609 Champlain made the grave mistake of challenging the Iroquois. Leading several dozen canoes loaded with Huron, Algonquin and Montagnais braves, he advanced into Five Nations territory to meet 200 Iroquois "men of men" in their distinctive elm-bark canoes. The war parties landed and lined up, facing each other. Champlain set up his arquebus and fired at the astonished warriors. That shot killed two Iroquois chiefs and wounded another, creating an enmity that would outlast New France. In the wars that followed, the braves of the Five Nations, armed now with "fire sticks" of their own, sided with the British to take their revenge.

In 1620 Champlain built a citadel above Lower Town, to ward off Iroquois attacks. His sketch of it (not the original log fortress he built upon his arrival) is shown on one of the stamps in the tercentenary issue of 1908. The stone fortress so impressed Iroquois spies that no native war parties ever attacked it. Yet, in 1629, when the British privateer Captain David Kirke anchored off Lower Town and demanded that Champlain surrender his colony,

1908 Champlain's Habitation

Champlain did so without firing a shot. He had only 16 emaciated men and 50 pounds of gunpowder with which to defend his fort.

Kirke had authority from Charles I to clear the French out of Canada. He loaded the inhabitants of Québec onto his ships and set sail for London. But when the privateer stepped ashore to present his king with his gifts — Canada, the founder of Québec and most of its population — he was astonished to learn that his conquest had been illegal. Peace had been signed between England and France.

Three years later Charles I sold Canada back to France for the equivalent of $240,000 — money owed to him from the dowry of his French wife. Champlain returned to Québec, reclaimed his colony and rebuilt his citadel. He was 66 and worn out by years of arguing with Paris, scheming and fighting with Indians and suffering through the harsh winters. He died on Christmas Day, 1635, in a bleak room in his fortress.

1960

In the spring of 1660, Adam Dollard, Sieur des Ormeaux, led a handful of French volunteers against hundreds of attacking Iroquois and saved the people of Montréal from massacre.

He was 25, recently arrived from France and an officer with the Montréal garrison, when news came that the Iroquois were on the warpath and heading for the town. He gathered 16 young men to help him ward off the attack. They made their wills, confessed their sins, said their prayers, and set off in birchbark canoes to intercept the attackers on the Ottawa River. Most of them had never paddled a canoe before.

At the Long Sault rapids they were ambushed and took shelter in an abandoned palisade. For a week they, with 40 friendly Indians, held out against the Iroquois. When their food and water were gone, Dollard's men threw a keg of gunpowder at the attackers, but it blew up too early and wounded many of them. The Iroquois then stormed the fort and massacred the defenders. Dollard was among the first to die. By their sacrifice, Dollard and his men delayed the attack on Montréal and saved the city.

20

The man who put New France on a business footing was a pleasant young bureaucrat with a twirly mustache — Jean Talon. When he arrived in Québec, the governor and the bishop were squabbling over how to run the colony. Talon moved in to restore order and to ensure that the colony prospered.

On his stamp the Great Intendant is shown posing with a newly married couple and the gifts bestowed upon them by the king — a cow and a bull, a hog and a sow, a hen and a rooster, a barrel of salt pork and a fat bag of coins. For Talon is perhaps best remembered for arranging to have shiploads of girls sent from France as prospective brides for the colonists. When they arrived, the *filles du roi*, or daughters of the king, would line up on the dock at Québec, ready to be married on the spot. Those not chosen for marriage by the men of Québec City might be shipped upstream to Trois-Rivières and Montréal to try their luck there. (Québec City women gained the reputation of being the fairest in New France.)

1962 Jean Talon, Québec's Great Intendant.

Talon expanded the colony, and a great governor came later to build on his work. Louis de Buade, Comte de Frontenac, shared Champlain's vision. He backed explorers such as La Salle and Daniel Greysolen, Sieur du Luth. He awed the Iroquois by his imperious presence, his great jutting jaw and his flowery language, which they loved. He called them his children instead of the usual term, "brothers," and they called him *Onontio*, father. For a time they buried the tomahawk.

1972 Frontenac, Governor of New France.

Frontenac's first term as governor (1672-82) was a great period in the history of New France. His second (1689-98) was probably the greatest. In the years between he languished in France, recalled by the king after having lost a fight with Bishop Laval. Frontenac was sent back to the colony because it had declined dramatically in his absence and a new war with the Iroquois, fiercer than anything seen before, had begun. Though 70 years of age, Frontenac was still as strong as the Rock of Québec and the only man capable of uniting the feuding colonists.

With the Iroquois threatening to wipe out the colony, he launched surprise attacks on the British New Englanders and New Yorkers, whom he blamed for the Iroquois uprising. This raised morale but brought retaliation.

In 1690 a British fleet under Sir William Phips — 32 vessels carrying over 2,000 men — arrived at Québec expecting to repeat Kirke's easy victory over Champlain. A junior British officer came ashore under a flag of truce to demand surrender. He was led blindfolded through the narrow streets of Lower Town and up to the stone fortress, Frontenac's lair. The blindfold was removed, and he stood there facing the great men of New France, which was then at its peak of power and glory. In addition to the silks, lace and powdered wigs, the messenger saw the hard, lined faces of men who had beaten the wilderness. But Frontenac dominated them all.

1959 Plains of Abraham

1908 Montcalm and Wolfe

He glared at the British officer and threw his note to the floor. "I will answer your general," he growled, "only by the mouths of my cannon."

Phips bombarded the city and tried to storm it but he was beaten off and went home.

A generation later, the supermen of New France were gone and the French regime was sinking in corruption toward its final defeat by the British. On September 13, 1759, General James Wolfe scaled the cliffs to the Plains of Abraham above Québec City and, after a pitched battle, defeated the French commander Louis-Joseph, Marquis de Montcalm. Both leaders died. The 1959 stamp commemorating the battle stresses not the conflict but the subsequent peace that brought about a bicultural nation. The British lion and the French fleur-de-lys support a banner emblazoned "Canada." A 1908 stamp bears a portrait of Montcalm, from a picture owned by his family in France, and of Wolfe, from a sketch made during the campaign by his aide-de-camp, Captain Hervey Smyth.

New France was less successful as a colony than the English settlements to the south. It was also less stable because so many of its men preferred the woods and life as *coureurs de bois* over farming or taking up a trade. After the conquest there were only 70,000 French Canadians left to rub elbows with two million British colonial inhabitants.

1930 Grand Pré

Another 10,000 French Canadians who had settled in the colony of Acadia, which covered present-day Nova Scotia, New Brunswick, much of the Gaspé Peninsula and part of the state of Maine, had been rounded up and deported to the American colonies in one of the most tragic events in the history of this nation. Their expulsion was immortalized in Longfellow's poem *Evangeline*, and the heroine's home of Grand Pré became the subject of a 1930 stamp.

1973 Pictou Settlers

Some of the Acadians eventually made their way back to Canada, but they discovered that others — mostly Yankees and Scotsmen — had moved in to claim their land. The immigration of the Scottish Highlanders to Nova Scotia began with the landing of the brig *Hector* at Pictou on September 15, 1773, an event which was commemorated on a stamp 200 years later.

The Highlanders had left their homeland behind because conditions in Scotland had become impossible. After 1746, when rebel clansmen led by Charles Edward Stuart (Bonnie Prince Charlie) were butchered by the English at Culloden, the clan system had fallen apart and an ancient way of life had ended. Kilts, plaids and bagpipes were outlawed. The clan chiefs, turning against their own people, had cleared off the impoverished tenants to make way for more profitable sheep. Oppressed and starving, the Highlanders had boarded overladen, fever-ridden ships for North America. At Pictou they proudly put on the kilts they had smuggled out of Scotland and followed a piper onto the shores of "New Scotland." This is the moving scene depicted on the commemorative stamp.

The Paris Treaty of 1783, which ended the American War of Independence and established the boundaries of the United States, brought a new flood of settlers to Canada. They were the United Empire Loyalists, people who had remained loyal to Britain during the war. About 50,000 of them headed north to seek refuge in what was left of British territory in North America. Some settled in Nova Scotia, others went to what would later become the provinces of New Brunswick, Ontario and Québec.

1985

Louis Hébert, apothecary and physician, was the nation's first true homesteader. Champlain brought him over from Paris in 1617 and gave him 10 acres outside the settlement, on the plains above. After taking one look at the dismal sheds of Lower Town, Hébert decided that he and his family could not stay there. He led them up the steep path to his new property, and the family spent its first night in Québec under a tree.

The next day Hébert began building a wooden house, which was replaced by a stone one. Around it he planted the apple trees and vegetables that would save his family and the other colonists from scurvy in winter. He was the first pharmacist in Québec, and the stamp which commemorates Hébert was issued in conjunction with an international convention of pharmacists in Montréal in 1985. It shows some of Hébert's medicinal plants and his mortar, as well as his scythe.

Later he acquired a neighbor, river pilot Abraham Martin, known as Maitre Abraham, who cleared the plateau beside the Hébert farm. Abraham is remembered as the owner of a battlefield, the Plains of Abraham.

Hébert prospered and was given a minor title; his family line continues to this day in Québec City.

1934 Loyalists

1984 Loyalists

A stamp issued in 1934 to commemorate the arrival of the Loyalists is taken from a bronze monument by Sydney March, which stands outside the Wentworth County courthouse in Hamilton, Ontario. It depicts the moment in the life of a Loyalist when he has drawn a lot for a piece of land and he and his wife are looking forward with hope, but some apprehension, to their new life in Canada.

In 1984, two hundred years after the Loyalists' arrival, another stamp was issued. It shows a family set against a background of the Grand Union flag, used by Britain from 1606 to 1801.

1983

The final stop of the Underground Railroad, which smuggled black slaves from the American South to freedom in Canada, was Dresden, Ontario. The leader of this fugitive community was the Reverend Josiah Henson. His determined gaze was captured in this handsome 1983 stamp on the 100th anniversary of his death.

Henson was born into slavery in Maryland in 1789. He arrived in Canada via the Underground Railway in 1830, then guided hundreds more black men and women across the Niagara River, dodging American slave-hunting gangs.

*In 1850 Henson risked arrest by returning to the United States to meet Harriet Beecher Stowe. She listened to his story, then modelled the character Uncle Tom in her novel **Uncle Tom's Cabin** on Henson. He returned to found a church, a school and a cooperative settlement around Dresden. He died there, aged 94, and "Uncle Tom" was carved on his gravestone. At the time the term had not acquired the meaning of subservience that it later took on.*

Henson was tough, often dictatorial, and very much in command of the flocks he shepherded to freedom.

At the time when the great Loyalist immigration took place, much of the western continent was privately owned. Rupert's Land covered the prairies to the Rocky Mountains, including parts of Minnesota and the Dakotas, as well as the northlands around Hudson Bay. This private empire belonged to the Hudson's Bay Company, which had made no effort to settle it. As the company's royal charter gave it all the rivers and surrounding land flowing into the bay, and many of these remained to be discovered, the company didn't even know how large its empire was.

Thomas Douglas, Earl of Selkirk, would change this. To help his fellow Scots, dispossessed by their lairds and chiefs, he had settled small colonies on Prince Edward Island and in southwestern Ontario. He later heard tales of unlimited rich black earth in Manitoba and saw that this might be a Promised Land for his poor crofters. To win support for his colonization project, Selkirk bought shares in the Hudson's Bay Company and then convinced its management to back his settlement. The company sold him 116,000 square miles of land for just 10 shillings.

1962 Lord Selkirk

In September 1811, the first 150 Selkirk immigrants sailed in through Hudson Bay, camped for the winter on the Nelson River, then boated to a bend in the Red River, below Lake Winnipeg. They built their first huts and tried to set up a farming community. The commemorative stamp shows the earl and, in the background, a solitary farmer who is wearing the once-forbidden kilt and sowing seed.

Three years later these settlers were driven out by Métis plainsmen, descendants of the French voyageurs and their Indian wives, and by traders for the Bay Company's rival, the North West Company. The Métis — described by the settlers as half-French, half-Indian and half-devil — feared that farming would ruin their fur trade. The Red River Settlement was looted and burned. Fighting between the farmers and North West traders raged until Selkirk arrived with a company of Swiss soldiers, veterans of the 1812 War. The attackers withdrew.

Selkirk laid out a new village, Kildonan, which later became Winnipeg, and permanent settlement of the West began.

1974 Winnipeg Centenary Issue

Chapter Three

The Leaders

1935 Fathers of Confederation

The union of the British North American provinces was born at Charlottetown, Prince Edward Island, in 1864. This momentous gathering was celebrated on a 1935 stamp, which showed the 25 men who attended the Charlottetown Conference, 22 of whom were to become Fathers of Confederation.

The meeting that hammered out the details of the union was held one month later, in Québec City. This gathering of the Fathers of Confederation had been depicted on a stamp even earlier, in 1917. Taken from Robert Harris's famous 1883 painting of the Québec Conference, which showed 34 delegates, the stamp was trimmed at the sides to show only 26 of them. Ten years later a stamp showing the full complement of delegates in the original Harris painting was issued. It was perhaps too full, because historians argue that only 33 delegates were present in Québec.

1917 Fathers of Confederation

1927 Fathers of Confederation

One of the strongest supporters of Confederation — and the dominant figure in these stamps — is John Alexander Macdonald, wily leader of the Ontario Tories. Known as "Old Tomorrow," from his habit of putting off decisions until the time was right, John A. was a visionary in the guise of a congenial tippler. His drinking bouts, brought on by family tragedies, were gleefully denounced in the Toronto *Globe*, founded and edited by his remorseless enemy George Brown, a fellow Scot. Still, as John A. boasted, the public preferred Macdonald drunk to Brown sober.

1968 George Brown

Brown, as his 1968 stamp shows, was a dour, lantern-jawed man. He was the leader of the Clear Grits, early Liberals who described themselves as "all sand and no dirt, clear grit all the way through." He and Macdonald had suspended their feud by the time they went to London together to negotiate British approval of a self-governing Canada. They watched the Epsom Derby, over a picnic basket and bottles of champagne, and rode home, standing on the carriage seats, and happily firing at pedestrians with peashooters.

Meanwhile, back in Nova Scotia, Confederation was in trouble. Its earliest supporter, the great Joseph Howe, had turned against it because Macdonald's ally Charles Tupper was getting all the local glory.

1973 Joseph Howe

1927 Sir John A. Macdonald

Confederation was saved by armed invasion from the United States. When a band of wild Irishmen called Fenians crossed the Niagara River near Fort Erie and announced that they had come to liberate Canadians from the British yoke, the Canadians declined the invitation. Determined, the Fenian leader led his men in a couple of skirmishes that left nine Canadian militiamen dead. Thousands of Canadians then descended upon the Fenians, yelling for blood. Realizing that the country was not ripe for republicanism, the Fenians retired across the river. But the raid jolted the provinces into action. United by anti-Americanism, the Maritimes swung back to Confederation, the British Parliament passed the British North America Act and, on July 1, 1867, the new nation was born.

Macdonald, now Sir John A., won the first national election for his Conservative Party and became prime minister at the age of 52.

1935 Mounted Police

1982 RCMP Constable

The classic Mountie stamp of 1935 was reproduced as a "stamp on a stamp" in 1982, more than a century after the North West Mounted Police force was established. It shows a lone officer on the prairies. He is obviously on regular duty, for he's not wearing the ceremonial red jacket shown on the Musical Ride stamp.

The Mounties' first ride en masse was an expedition which set out from southern Manitoba in the summer of 1874 to enforce the law over 2.5 million square miles of Western Canada. About 200 Mounties stemmed the second Riel Rebellion of 1885. Although greatly outnumbered, their scarlet-coated presence prevented the uprising from becoming more serious.

They wore pillbox hats, not the present wide-brimmed ones. Some of them went on to police the 1898 Klondike Gold Rush and maintain order over an ever-larger area, but they seldom rode in large groups. It was the individual officer, the lone Mountie portrayed on the stamp, that symbolized Canadian law.

1970 Louis Riel

Two years after Confederation, the new nation suddenly tripled in size when it purchased Rupert's Land from the Hudson's Bay Company for 300,000 pounds. Overnight, Macdonald became landlord of the entire West up to the Rocky Mountains. When he tried to send a lieutenant-governor and some troops into the territory to govern it, Louis Riel and his armed band of Métis turned them back.

The Métis, fearful they would lose any claim to the western lands they had settled, were rebelling. They chose as their leader Louis Riel, whose fiery determination is captured on a 1970 stamp. Traitor or hero, Riel changed the course of Western Canadian history.

South of the border, the United States army was poised to move in and "restore order" — in other words, to annex the Canadian Northwest. To prevent this Macdonald sent out a powerful figure to make peace with Riel, Donald Smith. Later Lord Strathcona, the principal shareholder of the Canadian Pacific Railway, Smith was then a director of the Hudson's Bay Company. Influential as he was, he failed in his mission because a rambunctious Ontario Orangeman, Thomas Scott, was shot by a Métis firing squad. Ontario was outraged, and thousands of British and Canadian troops rushed west to put down Riel's rebellion. They captured his headquarters at Fort Garry (Winnipeg), but the rebel leader escaped.

1970 Donald Alexander Smith, first a director of the Hudson's Bay Company, later principal shareholder of the Canadian Pacific Railway.

Macdonald didn't want Riel caught — he even offered him money to stay out of Canada — but Riel returned. He was elected to Parliament and later spent time in an insane asylum, before heading back West to launch his second rebellion. In 1885, at Duck Lake, north of Regina, Riel's 500 horsemen routed a squad of mounted policemen and volunteers, killing a dozen men before nearly 6,000 soldiers arrived to put down the uprising and arrest its leader.

Old, tired and testy, Macdonald then made the biggest mistake of his career. "Riel shall hang," he growled, "though every dog in Québec should bark in his favour." Within days after Riel died on the gallows at Regina, he had become a French hero and a Roman Catholic martyr. Macdonald and the Conservative Party lost the support of Québec, though Macdonald remained Prime Minister until his death in 1891.

The next great leader to spark the loyalty and the imaginations of Canadians from coast to coast was Wilfrid Laurier. This Liberal from Québec stepped into the office of prime minister in 1896. Queen Victoria, whose empire was at its peak, celebrated her Diamond Jubilee the following year. The queen's subjects came from every corner of the world to pay her homage. Three million people lined the streets of London to watch the colonial procession, which was headed by the stately prime minister of Canada, Sir Wilfrid Laurier, and his lady. Laurier had conquered London society with his dignity, charm and stream of oratory in perfect English. Peers and statesmen wooed this natural aristocrat from the colonies.

1927 Laurier and Macdonald

"We were dined and wined by royalty and aristocracy and plutocracy," Laurier wrote. "It is hard to stand up against the

1927 Sir Wilfrid Laurier

flattery of a gracious duchess." He soon learned the reasons for such treatment: Britain planned an imperial super-parliament in London and wanted Canada's unconditional military support in her colonial wars, plus a $35 million contribution toward new battleships. But Laurier stood up to the flattery. He killed the super-parliament idea, waffled on military support and offered no money for the Royal Navy — Canada would have its own navy instead.

Having spent his high school years in the all-Scottish village of New Glasgow, Québec, Laurier understood the thinking of the *anglais*. His party had grown out of the abortive 1837 rebellion against British rule led by Louis-Joseph Papineau, but Laurier wanted greater Québec representation inside, rather than outside, Canada. He steered the Liberals away from republicanism and the drift toward union with the States. Like all great Canadian prime ministers, Laurier was a compromiser.

He sent 7,000 Canadian volunteers to fight for Britain against the Boers in South Africa — too few, according to the Leader of the Opposition, and 7,000 too many in the view of Quebec nationalists. He passed his naval bill, which provided for five cruisers and six destroyers, despite Tory scorn and savage attack from Québec. And he founded an external affairs department.

Then he went too far. He supported "reciprocity," a free-trade deal offered by the United States, and all sides turned on him. "I am branded in Québec as a traitor to the French," he complained, "and in Ontario as a traitor to the English. In Québec I am branded as a jingo and in Ontario as a separatist. In Québec I am attacked as an imperialist and in Ontario as an anti-imperialist. I am neither, I am a Canadian."

In 1911 this great Canadian went down in defeat over free trade.

1951 Robert Borden

His successor, Robert Borden, led Canada through one of the biggest challenges the young nation had yet faced — the Great War. Borden's insistence that Canada be consulted about the progress of the war — there were close to half a million Canadians in the field — resulted in an invitation to attend the Imperial War Conference of 1917. There Borden teamed up with South Africa's Jan Christiaan Smuts to demand full recognition of the dominions as autonomous nations. Surprisingly, Britain agreed. This would lead to the Declaration of 1926 and the Statute of Westminster (1931), which gave Canada effective control of its affairs at home and abroad. After the war Borden won Canada a place at the peace table and a seat in the new League of Nations.

1961 Arthur Meighen

Borden was succeeded by Arthur Meighen, who had two short periods as prime minister — the second (1926) was so short that he was never even sworn in. His brilliant and ambitious rival, William Lyon Mackenzie King, the young leader of the Liberal Party, outfoxed Governor General Lord Byng and pulled off a constitutional caper that saw Meighen shuffled to the sidelines of power.

In all his portraits, including his stamp portrait, King appears to be a mild and somewhat dumpy man. But his quiet demeanor disguises a most unusual character. King was the grandson of William Lyon Mackenzie, the rebel who fought for responsible government in 1837, escaped to the United States disguised as an old woman and, after his pardon, returned to Toronto. King considered his life an extension of his grandfather's, and he communicated with the ghost of the man through his mother. In later years Canadians were to discover that King had apparently used the advice of ghosts and spiritualist mediums to govern the country, but during his long career as the leader of the Liberals, much of it as prime minister, few were aware of this. In fact, King had a reputation for conveying nothing; most of the time this is exactly what he wanted to convey.

1951 William Lyon Mackenzie King

1971

On October 10, 1970, Québec's Labor Minister, Pierre Laporte, was seized by hooded gunmen outside his Montréal home. This second kidnapping by the separatist Front de Libération du Québec (FLQ) *triggered the introduction of martial law in Canada under the War Measures Act and the arrest of 400 people without warrant.*

Four terrorists kept Laporte handcuffed in a small Montréal house. He tried to escape by smashing his way through a window, but the kidnappers pulled him back. Later Laporte was found strangled by the gold chain and religious medal he wore around his neck.

One year later this tragic event, and Laporte's contribution to Canada, were recalled on the Pierre Laporte stamp.

King slipped up in 1930 when, after four years as prime minister, he made an election speech that did say something. It cost him the election. At the time Canada was plunged into the Great Depression, and the provincial premiers were begging for federal aid for their unemployed. King said he might give some to the provinces with Progressive governments but "not one five-cent piece" to any Tory government!

From then on, every election speech he made was drowned out by hecklers shouting "Five-cent piece!" The jobless and shoeless turned out in droves to vote for Richard Bedford Bennett, a Tory multimillionaire whose shoes, a reporter wrote, "not only glisten but gloat."

When he took office in 1930, Bennett inherited a land of misery, hoboes, soup-kitchens and "Bennett buggies" — derelict automobiles pulled by horses. About the only good thing he inherited was the Statute of Westminster, the work of his predecessors, which he signed in 1931. This gave Canada virtual independence from Britain. But Bennett failed to find a way to end the Depression, and the country never forgave him. He lost the 1935 election to Mackenzie King, who campaigned on the slogan "King or Chaos."

1955 Richard Bedford Bennett

King looked south of the border where Franklin Roosevelt's New Deal policies, by which the U.S. government was pumping money into its economy, were having a positive effect. He timidly considered a similar policy for Canada, but then came World War Two, the great challenge to the newly independent nation and its prime minister.

King worked with Churchill to bring America into the war, acting as the go-between for him and Roosevelt. He brought the country through another conscription crisis under the baffling slogan "Conscription if necessary, but not necessarily conscription." He presided over Canada's staggering industrial expansion which ripped through the predominantly rural nation in about two years.

After the war King remained in power when Roosevelt was dead and Churchill was out of office. He planted the seeds of future social welfare programs and introduced Canadian citizenship. (Before July 1, 1947, Canadians were British subjects.)

King chose as his successor Louis Stephen St. Laurent, who held on as prime minister for another nine years. But in 1957 Canadians decided that 22 years of Liberal government was enough and elected a fiery Conservative from the prairies.

1974 Louis Stephen St. Laurent

John George Diefenbaker, whose famous jowls were captured on a stamp in 1980, one year after his death, had spent a lifetime on the losing side of politics. It made him a splendid parliamentary attacker, but he had never had to defend himself. In his first term as minority leader, nobody noticed because he was a great actor of the old school, and Canadians were ready for greatness. He championed the underdog because he had been one himself. He brought in his Bill of Rights. He drove racist South Africa out of the Commonwealth at the cost of alienating Britain. Later, he balanced this by alienating the United States as well.

Just 18 months into his term as prime minister, the Liberals offered Dief a spectacular excuse to dissolve Parliament and win a huge majority. Their new leader, Lester Pearson, made the timid suggestion that Diefenbaker resign and hand the government back to the Liberals. Even as he spoke, Pearson seemed to realize his mistake.

The prime minister rose to his full height, waggled his jowls and proceeded to lambaste the rookie opposition leader for two hours. He unleashed his Vision upon Canadians. "I see a new land," he intoned, "a Canada of the North! Jobs! A new Vision! A new Hope! A new Soul for Canada!" Diefenbaker's Vision, though it had few concrete results, inspired people as no actual project could. It was a dream, a myth, but it worked — until dollars and a warplane brought it to an end.

1980 John George Diefenbaker

The governor of the Bank of Canada said Canada was living beyond its means. There was a screaming row and Diefenbaker resigned. Investors lost confidence, capital poured out of Canada and the dollar was suddenly devalued to 92.5 cents. In the 1962 election, Liberals distributed "Diefendollars," bills bearing a maniacal face of the leader, with dotted lines showing where seven and a half cents had been cut off the bill. The Tories squeaked back into office with a minority.

The warplane that brought Diefenbaker's dream crashing down around him was the Avro CF 105 *Arrow* interceptor, possibly the greatest triumph of the Canadian aviation industry. Diefenbaker had cancelled construction of it and put 14,000 employees out of work. The *Arrow* was the most advanced aircraft of its time, but the bill to produce it had grown too expensive for Canada — and the Americans would not buy this Canadian-made plane. But Canada still needed to fulfill its responsibilities in North American air defence, and so Diefenbaker bought American equipment, including *Bomarc B* missiles designed to carry nuclear warheads. Diefenbaker would not accept the warheads because American troops came with them. (All U.S. nuclear weapons had to be guarded by Americans.)

Early in 1963 the Kennedy administration accused Canada of failing in its defence duties. When Diefenbaker denied this, the State Department issued a press release that all but called him a liar. Diefenbaker's Cabinet split, the opposition parties ganged up on him and his government was defeated in the House.

Lester Pearson won the election that followed. He is perhaps best remembered for giving the country its distinctive maple leaf flag, though he was also the first Canadian to win the Nobel Peace Prize. Pearson bowed out gracefully at the end of 1967 — Centennial Year — the last of the government leaders to be commemorated on a stamp.

1972 Lester B. Pearson, Prime Minister and winner of the Nobel Peace Prize.

Chapter Four

Kings and Queens

The portrait of a reigning monarch lends authority to a stamp. He or she is the highest figure in the land and is responsible, in theory at least, for the service the stamp guarantees. So the Royal Mail used royal stamps and so do its successors.

The original Penny Black (1840) carried a profile of Queen Victoria, sculpted when she was 18 years old. That profile was still in use on some stamps after she died at 82, although stamps bearing her portrait at a more mature age had been issued. These include the "widow's weeds" picture, which she chose herself to emphasize her long mourning for her consort, Prince Albert. When he died she went into seclusion in her castles and refused to meet her subjects. This led to resentment against Victoria, but when she finally emerged from her grief, and began to rule her rapidly expanding empire, her millions of subjects lavished loyalty on her. None were more loyal than Canadians.

A Canadian stamp portraying both the young queen of 1837 and the older one of 60 years later shows not the ravages of time but the wisdom of age.

Victoria was more than a constitutional monarch and a symbol of Empire. She demanded that her governments carry out the policies she had approved, without changing them. And, when they couldn't make up their minds, she made decisions for them. It was she who decided that neither Toronto nor Montréal but the little lumbering centre of Bytown (later named Ottawa) would be the capital of a united Dominion. She never saw her young capital because she never visited Canada.

Royal visits began with her son, the Prince of Wales, later Edward VII, who made a triumphal tour of Canada in 1860. At Niagara Falls he watched Blondin, the great tightrope walker, perform on his wire over the gorge. Blondin offered to carry him across the river on his back, but the young prince graciously declined.

Do royals collect stamps bearing their pictures? Yes, indeed. George V started the Royal Stamp Collection that is now

1893 Queen Victoria, in her widow's weeds.

1897 Jubilee Double Portrait showing Queen Victoria at aged 18 and 78.

1965 View of the Parliament Buildings

1928 George V

1903 Edward VII

1935 Edward, Prince of Wales, who gave up the throne to marry Wallis Simpson.

1939 Princesses Elizabeth and Margaret

1951 Duchess and Duke of Edinburgh

cared for by Queen Elizabeth II, who began collecting stamps as a girl.

George V, the Sailor King, was more than just an ardent philatelist; while Prince of Wales he co-designed the definitive Canadian stamp series showing his father, Edward VII. The Sailor King's pictures, including his favorite ones in naval uniform, appear on hundreds of stamps.

The future Edward VIII toured Canada just after the Great War and returned in 1927 to represent George V at Canada's Diamond Jubilee celebrations in Ottawa. He is commemorated as Prince of Wales. A Canadian stamp showing him as king was prepared and ready to print in 1936, when he gave up the throne to marry "the woman I love," American divorcee Wallis Simpson. The dies were destroyed, although one version of the unissued stamp is preserved in Ottawa.

The first reigning monarch to visit Canada was George VI, who came with his Queen Elizabeth, now the Queen Mother, and their two little princesses, Elizabeth and Margaret Rose. Their 1939 royal progress is still remembered for the surge of patriotic feeling it generated. It was then, on the eve of the Second World War, that the King unveiled Ottawa's memorial to the dead of the First World War. Designed by Vernon March, of Kent, it is a 60-foot granite arch through which pass 19 bronze figures representing units of the Canadian Forces.

The present Queen and her consort, Prince Philip, come here often, so a royal tour is no longer the unique occasion it was in 1939. But, from coast to coast and high in the Arctic, the crowds and the enthusiasm are still strong.

According to the *Guinness Book of Records*, the present Queen has her picture on more stamps than anyone else. By 1988 she had appeared on 8,739 different issues. Canada has portrayed her at different ages, from 6 to over 60, and is the only country to have portrayed her as Princess Elizabeth, Duchess of Edinburgh.

1973 James E.H. MacDonald's *Mist Fantasy*

1973 RCMP Centenary Issue

1977 saw the issue of Tom Thompson's paintings, *April in Algonquin Park* (above) and *Autumn Birches* (below).

1988 issue of Canadian Butterflies depicts (clockwise) Macoun's Arctic, Canadian Tiger Swallowtails, Short-tailed Swallowtail, and the Northern Blue.

Québec, Adrien Hébert

Yukon Territory, A.Y. Jackson

Newfoundland, Christopher Pratt

Northwest Territories, René Richard

Prince Edward Island, Molly Lamb

Saskatchewan, Dorothy Knowles

To celebrate Canada Day in 1982, scenes painted by Canadian artists were rendered on a series of stamps.

Nova Scotia, Alex Colville

Ontario, David Milne   Alberta, Illingworth Kerr   British Columbia, Joe Plaskett

Manitoba, Lionel Le Moine Fitzgerald

New Brunswick, Bruno Bobak

Canada's explorers have been commemorated on a number of beautiful issues.

1986 Vikings **1986 John Cabot**

1987 Wilderness Missionaries

1986 First Peoples

1987 Joliette and Marquette

1986 Henry Hudson

Canada Day 1981 saw the issue of a series of stamps of maps showing the country's evolution.

1988 George Vancouver

Canada in 1867

1988 Simon Fraser

Canada in 1873

Canada in 1905

Canada since 1949

Fort Walsh, Saskatchewan

Fort York, Ontario

Castle Hill, Newfoundland

Fort Anne, Nova Scotia

Fort Lennox, Québec

Fort Erie, Ontario

Fort Whoop Up, Alberta

In 1985 the forts of Canada were illustrated on stamps as a tribute to the role they played in both our civilian and military history.

York Redoubt, Nova Scotia

Fort Frederick, Ontario

Lower Fort Garry, Manitoba

1979 Bowhead whale, painted by Robert Bateman

1953 Polar Bear

1988 Killer Whale

1988 Lynx

1953 Moose

1988 Wapiti

1981 Vancouver Island Marmot, painted by Michael Dumas

1955 Whooping Crane

1952 Canada Goose

1977 Eastern Cougar, painted by Robert Bateman

1989 Grizzly Bear

1989 Musk Ox

1980 Greater Prairie Chicken, painted by Robert Bateman

From the first stamp issued — the Threepence Beaver — the animals and birds of Canada have provided inspiration to stamp designers.

45

Canada's aboriginal people have been the subject of many stamps. The popularity of Inuit carvings, for instance, led to a rediscovery of their pictorial art, represented on stamps in hunting and fishing scenes, recreations of Inuit spirits and a brilliant print evoking the annual joy of the Return of the Sun.

1980 Inuit Shaman

1979 Inuit Dance

1977 Inuit Fisherman

1977 Inuit Archer

1976 Iroquoian Couple

1980 Inuit *Return of the Sun*

Inuit artists represented here include Simon Tookoone, Kalvak, Kenojouak, Pitseolak, Abraham and Pudlo.

1979 Inuit *Summer Tent*

1978 *Airplane* over Inuit village

1978 Inuit *Woman Walking*

1978 *Dogsled*

1977 Inuit Seal Hunter

1976 Iroquoian Thunderbird

1976 Iroquoian Encampment

1978 Inuit *Migration*

1979 Inuit Soapstones from Repulse Bay

1976 Iroquoian Artifacts

1980 Inuit *Bird Spirit*

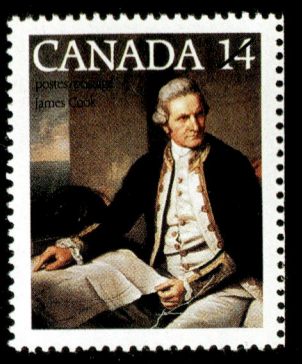

1978 Captain James Cook, who charted Canada's west coast in a vain attempt to find the elusive Northwest Passage.

1971 *Indian Encampment on Lake Huron* by Paul Kane, issued on the 100th anniversary of the painter's death.

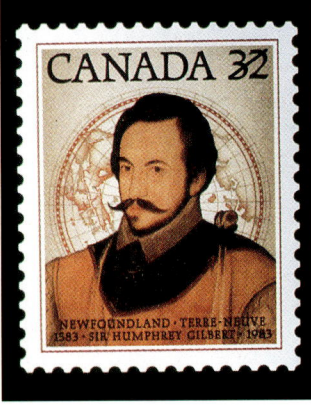

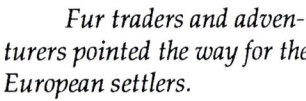

1983 Sir Humphrey Gilbert

1968 *Nonsuch* marked the 300th anniversary of Hudson's voyage.

Fur traders and adventurers pointed the way for the European settlers.

1987 Pierre-Esprit Radisson and Sieur des Groseilliers, *coureurs de bois*

1984 Étienne Brûlé

1973 Pictou Settlers

1971 Samuel Hearne

1985 Louis Hébert, Québec's first pharmacist

1983 Josiah Henson, leader of the fugitive slave community in Canada, at Dresden, Ontario.

1972 300th anniversary of Frontenac's appointment as Governor of New France.

1951 William Lyon Mackenzie King

1927 Sir John A. Macdonald

1927 Sir Wilfrid Laurier

1955 Richard Bennett

1982 RCMP Constable, showing the original stamp issued in 1935.

1951 Sir Robert Borden

1971 Pierre Laporte

Many of our outstanding citizens are represented on stamps.

1897 Issue on Queen Victoria's Diamond Jubilee

1897 Diamond Jubilee

1928 King George V

1928 King George V

1930 King George V

1903 King Edward VII

1935 Prince of Wales

1935 Princess Elizabeth

The portrait of a reigning monarch lends authority to a stamp.

1939 Princesses issue commemorating the royal visit.

1973 Elizabeth II

1951 Duchess and Duke of Edinburgh, commemorating the 1951 royal visit.

1981 Louise McKinney

1981 Idola Saint-Jean

1981 Henrietta Edwards

1980 Emma Albani, soprano

1971 *Big Raven* by Emily Carr

1981 Emily Stowe, Canada's first woman doctor.

1988 Frances Ann Hopkins, painter

1981 Marie de l'Incarnation

1973 Nellie McClung

1986 La Mauricie National Park, Quebec

1967 *Solemn Land* by J.E.H. MacDonald

1967 *Jack Pine* by Tom Thomson

1984 Glacier National Park

1967 *Alaska Highway* by A.Y. Jackson

1928 Mount Hurd

1930 Mount Edith Cavell

1982 Waterton Lakes National Park

1981 John Macoun, botanist

1979 Kluane National Park

1985 Banff National Park

1935 Niagara Falls

1970 *Isles of Spruce* by Arthur Lismer

1967 *Bylot Island* by Lawren Harris

1968 Inuit Carving

1955 Inuk and Kayak

1975 Kutchin Ceremonial Costume

1975 Ojibwa Thunderbird

1973 Algonkian Artifacts

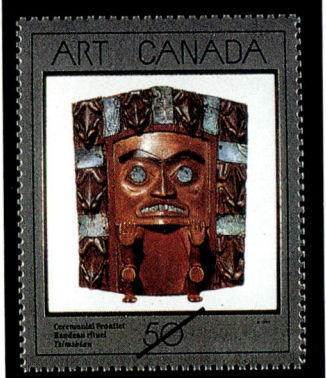

1989 Ceremonial Frontlet

1973 Algonkian Thunderbird

Native peoples produced reverently stylized representations of people and spirits, evoked in objects designed for both everyday and ceremonial use.

1956 Caribou

1989 Haida Canoe, carved from Pacific coast red cedars.

1956 Mountain Goat

1989 Micmac Canoe

1957 Loon

1989 Chipewyan Canoe

1989 Inuit Kayak

1959 Opening of the St. Lawrence Seaway

1959 50th Anniversary of the first flight in Canada by J.A. McCurdy's *Silver Dart*

Events and innovations in Canadian transportation have been commemorated on these stamps.

1986 Canada Day issue celebrated Science and Techonology in four stamps.

1986 Canadian Locomotive

1987 *Segwun* Steamship

1933 *Royal William*

1984 *Countess of Dufferin*

1935 Royal Yacht *Britannia*

1951 Stagecoach and Plane

1985 Canadian Locomotive

1986 Canadian Locomotive

1981 Avro Canada C-102

1928 Airmail

1930 Mercury Airmail

1981 de Havilland Canada *Dash-7*

1969 Vickers *Vimy* Atlantic Flight

1942 War Issue Airmail

1982 *Noorduyn Norseman*

1982 *Fokker Super Universal*

1966 issue of *Alouette II* commemorating its launch in 1965.

1980 issue depicting the 1935 Hawker *Hurricane*.

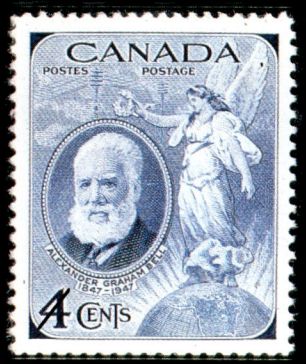

1947 Alexander Graham Bell

1974 stamp marks the centenary of the invention of the telephone.

1974 Marconi and Signal Hill

1978 Athabasca Tar Sands

1987 R.A. Fessenden

1987 F.N. Gisborne and the undersea cable

1987 G.E. Desbarats and W. Leggo

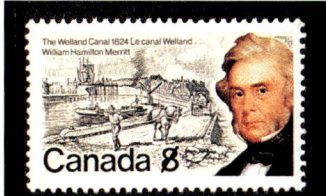

1974 William Merritt and the Welland Canal

1986 map of the site of the Calgary Winter Olympics

1976 Basketball

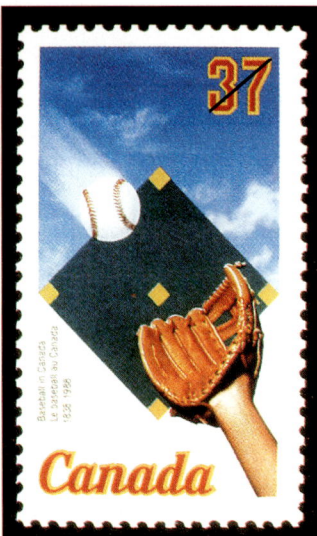

1982 Terry Fox and the Marathon of Hope

1975 Sailing

1975 Swimming

1976 Olympic Medal Ceremony

1976 Olympic Opening Ceremony

1988 Canadian Baseball

1929 *Bluenose*, Canada's most famous racing schooner.

1975 Pole Vault

1975 Marathon

1975 Hurdles

1979 issue marking the Canoe-Kayak World Championships, Jonquière, Québec.

1979 Women's Field Hockey

1978 Commonwealth Games Stadium

1974 Hiking

1974 Snowshoeing

1978 Commonwealth Games — Running

Chapter Five

Pioneering Women

Little is known about the earliest women settlers from Europe, except those who labored to provide religious, educational and medical care to the colonists. While the missionary priests ventured deep into the forests to convert the natives, the nuns stayed behind to bring peace and sanctity to the strife-ridden little settlements.

In Champlain's day, Mother Marie de l'Incarnation headed the first Ursuline convent in Québec, educating French and Indian girls. Though she did not teach Kateri Tekakwitha, both Canadian women were beatified by the Catholic Church in 1980, an event which was marked the following year with a stamp issue.

1981 Marie de l'Incarnation

Tekakwitha, also known as the Lily of the Mohawks, was the first North American Indian candidate for sainthood. In 1676, she accepted the Christian faith through baptism. For this her own people persecuted her, but after her death in 1680, many favors and miracles were attributed to her.

Sister Marguerite Bourgeoys arrived at Québec in 1653 and went on to Montréal to found the Congregation of Notre Dame, the first religious order to originate in Canada. She opened the first school in Montréal, an event which was commemorated on a 1975 stamp which depicts her teaching young girls how to read. She is now Saint Marguerite.

1981 Kateri Tekakwitha

Jeanne Mance, the first secular nurse to come to the colony, founded Montréal's first hospital, Hôtel-Dieu. Together with Sister Marguerite Bourgeoys, she was a devout and tireless worker for the well-being of her community.

The European women who settled in the New World labored in the shadow of men; they had no political rights and very few domestic rights. But, for some native women, life was very different. In the League of the Five (later Six) Nations, Iroquois chiefs descended matrilineally, and the matrons in each tribe were powerful figures.

As chief matron of the Iroquois, Molly Brant commanded the respect of her Mohawk tribesmen and of the British and American leaders.

1975 Sister Marguerite Bourgeoys

1973 Jeanne Mance, the first secular nurse in Canada.

1986 Molly Brant (Konwatsi Tsiaienni), Mohawk Princess.

1981 Emily Stowe, Canada's first female physician.

1981 Idola Saint-Jean, who helped to win the right for women to vote in provincial elections.

While still in her teens, she married William Johnson in a Mohawk ceremony. Johnson, a huge, unruly Irishman, had been shipped out to the colonies by his family and told not to come back. He became a British version of the *coureur de bois*, living among the natives, sometimes as a native. He obtained a huge tract of land in New York State and built a mansion, Johnson Hall. When war with the French began, he became Sir William Johnson and was charged with leading the Iroquois into battle.

Molly never used the title "Lady Johnson." She preferred to keep her Mohawk rank and Indian name, Konwatsi Tsiaienni, but she was the perfect British chatelaine of Johnson Hall, presiding at elaborate balls when not living in the smoky huts of her tribespeople. Like Sir William, she led a double life.

When he died in 1774, just as the American Revolution was about to begin, Molly assumed an authority equal to that of her brother, Joseph, then the paramount chief of the Mohawks. She rode from village to village with a tomahawk in her saddlebags, rousing the tribes to war for King George III. (Iroquois women did not take part in planned attacks but were known to fight in surprise ones.)

After the British defeat, she and Joseph led their people to new lands across the Niagara River in Ontario. They were among the first Loyalist colonizers of Upper Canada, a historical event which was brought to light again in 1986 when the Molly Brant commemorative stamp was issued.

Women's progress toward equality was slow during the pre-Confederation years. In the mid-1800s women were still not allowed to attend university. That changed after 1875, when the first female student enrolled at Mount Allison University.

Emily Stowe was one woman who didn't accept no for an answer. She obtained a university education, including a degree as a physician from a New York university, and became Canada's first female physician and school principal, two "firsts" which were recognized in a 1981 stamp. She had to practice medicine for 13 years, however, before she was granted her Canadian license, in 1880.

Stowe was also a leader in Canada's suffrage movement, having founded, in 1876, the Toronto Women's Literary Club. Its members were Canada's first suffragettes. The struggle for the right to vote was taken up by the Women's Christian Temperance Union (WCTU), which believed that female society would advance faster if men stopped drinking so much. The suffragette-prohibitionists waged a spirited campaign, but in general the struggle for the vote for women was less militant here than in Britain or the United States.

It took the Great War to bring women the vote. With so many men fighting overseas, many women had stepped into the jobs left vacant by the military recruits. Recognition of their equal status soon followed. In 1916 Manitoba, Saskatchewan and Alberta granted women the vote in provincial elections. British Columbia and Ontario followed in 1917. In that year, too, with passage of the Wartime Elections Act, wives of servicemen were allowed to vote in federal elections. Enfranchisement for all the women of Canada in federal elections came the following year, in 1918.

The other provinces held out longer — Québec for another 20 years, until 1940. Idola Saint-Jean was one of the women who were instrumental in winning the right for women to vote in provincial elections in Québec. Thérèse Casgrain, later Senator Casgrain, was a founding member of the Provincial Franchise Committee for women's suffrage in 1921, and of the League for Human Rights in 1960. The achievements of both women have been commemorated on stamps.

1985 Senator Thérèse Casgrain

But winning the right to vote was only one of the challenges that women faced. Until Judge Emily Murphy, the first woman magistrate in the British Empire, took her famous case to London, women were not considered "persons" in matters of legal rights and privileges. When her appointment as a judge was challenged on these grounds, she took the case to the Supreme Court of Alberta, which rejected the argument. But this was not good enough for Emily. She enlisted the support of four others to agitate for the appointment of a woman to the Senate. This meant petitioning Parliament for an interpretation of the word "persons" as used in the British North America Act. In 1928 the Supreme Court of Canada ruled that women were not "persons," so the five vanguard feminists carried their case to the final legal authority, the Privy Council in London. There they finally won women recognition as persons.

1985 Judge Emily Murphy, first woman magistrate in the British Empire.

Everyone expected that Emily Murphy would become the first female senator but, as a veteran senator put it, "Oh, we couldn't have Mrs. Murphy in the Senate! She would stir up too much trouble." So, in 1930, Cairine Wilson became the first woman appointed to the Senate.

1973 Nellie McClung

1981 Louise McKinney

1981 Henrietta Edwards

Agnes MacPhail was the first woman M.P. She entered the Commons in 1921 and stayed there for 19 years. Louise McKinney was elected to the Alberta Legislature as an Independent in 1917. She was also a world vice-president of the Women's Christian Temperance Union. Henrietta Edwards had a successful career as a women's reform activist and helped found the Victorian Order of Nurses. Irene Parlby was the first woman cabinet minister in a

1961 E. Pauline Johnson, Mohawk writer

provincial legislature. And Nellie McClung was a suffragette, prohibitionist and holy terror. McClung's slogan was "Never retract, never explain, never apologize — get the thing done and let them howl!"

In the arts, the stamp history of women begins with another Mohawk princess, E. Pauline Johnson, possibly a descendant of Molly Brant's husband, Sir William. Her father was Mohawk chief George Henry M. Johnson, her mother was English, and she was born on the Six Nations Reserve near Brantford, Ontario, in 1861. Her poems, which appeared in Canadian, American and English magazines in the late 1880s, presented a romantic view of Indian life. She gave stage recitals nationally and internationally, dressed in Mohawk costume. Later she moved to Vancouver to write stories about the legends and customs of the Pacific Coast tribes.

1971 Emily Carr, painter

Emily Carr, whose famous painting *Big Raven* was reproduced on a 1971 stamp, was born in Victoria in 1871. She sketched, painted and wrote about the natives of the Pacific Coast. She was one of the first white women to travel to remote coastal villages to record the beauty and majesty of native totem poles. The Indians called her *Klee Wyck*, the Laughing One.

1988 Frances Ann Hopkins, painter

Frances Ann Hopkins (1838-1918), whose portrait, as well as one of her best-known paintings (*Canoe Manned by Voyageurs*) is depicted on a 1988 stamp, also travelled into the wilderness to find inspiration for her art.

1980

One woman whose contribution to Canadian arts history is often overlooked is Emma Lajeunesse (1847-1930). Emma Albani, as she was known to her many fans, was the great operatic and oratorio singer of her period. Born in Chambly, Québec, she made a sensational London debut in 1872 and then went on to build an internationally acclaimed career.

Lucy Maud Montgomery turned her childhood memories into a famous story that made Prince Edward Island familiar to readers around the world. Born in Clifton, P.E.I., in 1874, Montgomery began writing children's stories while on the staff of the *Halifax Chronicle*. Her first book for girls was *Anne of Green*

Gables (1908). It recounts the tale of a determined orphan from Toronto who finds a home and security on a farm on P.E.I. The book was an instant success, and nearly 50 years later her little Anne, who is shown contemplating her future on a 1975 stamp, was still adventuring in television films and stage productions shown around the world.

1975 Lucy Maud Montgomery, writer

Chapter Six

The Environment

Stamps portraying individuals are always interesting, but for sheer beauty many Canadians turn to stamps that display the land itself. Early landscape stamps include ones picturing Mount Hurd, in the Rockies, Mount Edith Cavell, named after the heroic nurse of World War One, and Horseshoe Falls at Niagara, probably Canada's greatest natural phenomenon.

1928 Mount Hurd

None are more spectacular than the stamps that showcase seven of Canada's national parks.

1982 Banff National Park

1930 Mount Edith Cavell

Banff National Park, designated in 1885, is probably the most famous of all Canada's parks. It covers 6,640 square kilometres of terrain along the Continental Divide of the Rocky Mountains. Banff tells the geological story of the West — where mountains were squeezed up from the floor of an ancient sea, then carved by mile-thick glaciers, traces of which still cling to them. Glacial lakes abound. One of the best known, Lake Louise, gets its dazzling emerald color from the glacial sediment beneath its waters.

1935 Horseshoe Falls

Each spring the stark winter landscape of rock and ice gives way to a rugged garden of colors — the yellow of the columbine complementing the magenta fireweed and the blue clematis.

1984 Glacier National Park

Moose, elk, deer, beaver and about 60 other species of mammal live in the park, along with grizzly bears, perhaps the most feared of Canada's animals. For the most part the grizzlies stay out of sight, but a visitor to the park is likely to spot a black bear.

Farther west lies Glacier National Park, on the Selkirk Range, mountains which are millions of years older than the Rockies. They seemed impenetrable to early travelers, until an engineer working for the Canadian Pacific Railway discovered the pass named after him. For more than 70 years Rogers Pass was only

1962 Stamp issued on the opening of the Trans-Canada Highway, Rogers Pass.

1977 Kluane National Park

1982 Waterton Lakes

1986 La Mauricie

1988 St. Maurice Ironworks

1981 John Macoun

1967 *Bylot Island*, by Lauren Harris

accessible by rail, but in 1962 the Trans-Canada Highway also pushed its way through the Selkirks. A section of the highway boasts one of the world's heaviest snowfalls, so concrete sheds were built along it to protect cars from avalanches.

Kluane National Park, in the Yukon, is also mountainous. Canada's highest peak, Mount Logan (5,951 metres), presides over the park, which stretches across an area almost four times the size of Prince Edward Island. The park is home to giant mountain caribou and some of the largest moose on the continent. Silver City is in the park as well. Visitors to this genuine ghost town of the gold-panning days can still see rotting sluice boxes and cabins whose floorboards may have hidden bags of gold dust.

Waterton Lakes National Park, in Alberta, became the first international peace park in 1932 when it was linked with Glacier National Park in Montana. It features peculiar U-shaped valleys and canyons. The park is still home to a few bison, descendants of the millions that once roamed the prairies.

La Mauricie National Park occupies 544 square kilometres of land north of Shawinigan, Québec. This park, which has over 100 lakes, is home to beaver, moose, bear, lynx and wolves. Though now it attracts visitors because of its tranquility and seclusion, the area was once the centre of heavy industry for New France. A tall stone chimney is all that remains of Canada's first iron foundry, opened in 1730 to produce stoves, pots, tools and anchors from local ore. It was abandoned in 1883.

1979 Fundy National Park

1983 Point Pelée

The 1979 stamp of Fundy National Park shows the immense tide, the highest in the world, that surges along the park's shoreline. Rising above the shore are steep sandstone cliffs that lead to a rolling plateau of tree-shaded hills and bright, flowery meadows — southeastern New Brunswick at its best. This is Loyalist country, a place of old churches and an autumnal calm.

The gentlest of national parks is Point Pelée, which juts out on Lake Erie. This lush haven nurtures many spectacular flowers, including Canada's only wild hibiscus. Point Pelée lies in Canada's banana belt — one of the longest frost-free areas in the country — and many species of birds stop there while migrating. Some, including the great blue heron, the great horned owl and the saw-whet owl, even stay to nest. It is also the traditional stopover for the monarch butterflies that brighten the sky in autumn. These migrants have not been represented on a stamp, but four all-Canadian varieties of butterfly (and the botanist John Macoun who identified one variety of butterfly) have.

The artists of each generation who evoked the grandeur of scenic Canada are well represented on stamps, in particular those artists who have been associated with the Group of Seven. The painters who founded the group in 1920 sought their inspiration in Canada's North. Their work has been the source of particularly fine stamps such as *Bylot Island*, by Lawren Harris; *Isles of Spruce*, by Arthur Lismer; *The Solemn Land*, by J.E.H. MacDonald; and *Alaska Highway*, by A.Y. Jackson. Frederick Varley has his own issue, a self-portrait. Tom Thomson, who is always associated with the group but was not a member, is best remembered for his single pine tree in *The Jack Pine*.

1981 *Self-Portrait*, by Frederick Varley

In 1982, to mark Canada Day, a series on Canadian paintings was issued. Twelve artists, one for each province or territory, contributed their paintings, including Dorothy Knowles, of Saskatchewan, Alex Colville, of Nova Scotia, Christopher Pratt, of Newfoundland, and Adrien Hébert, of Québec.

1967 *The Jack Pine*, by Tom Thomson

An earlier era of landscape painting is evoked in Lucius O'Brien's tranquil painting *Sunrise on the Saguenay*. It was reproduced on a stamp in 1980, to mark the centennial of the National Gallery of Canada. This magnificent painting was one of the first works acquired by the gallery.

1970 *Isles of Spruce*, by Arthur Lismer

Other artists have contributed works which represent the nation's wildlife. In 1977 a series depicting endangered species of Canadian mammals, birds and fish was launched. Robert Bateman and Michael Dumas contributed works to this series, which shows eight endangered species from across the country.

From the days of Sir Sandford Fleming, who gave this nation its first animal stamp in 1851 — the Threepence Beaver — the animals and birds of Canada have provided inspiration to stamp designers. The musk ox, caribou, mountain goat and grizzly bear, the whooping crane, Canada goose, loon and prairie chicken have all been commemorated on a stamp.

1967 *Alaska Highway*, by A.Y. Jackson

Canada's environment has been an endless source of inspiration for artists, much of it captured on stamps.

1980 *Sunrise on the Saguenay*, by Lucius O'Brien

Chapter Seven

First Peoples

Canada's first people migrated from Asia, across the frozen Bering Strait, about 30,000 years ago. The earliest migrants went south to the plains. As the glaciers receded, some people headed eastward toward the Atlantic, and others, the Inuit, moved back north. The Indians formed distinct territorial groups — those of the Pacific Northwest, the Subarctic, the Plains and the eastern confederacies of the Algonkian and Iroquoian.

With these divisions came different languages, different ways of living on and working the land and different forms of artistic expression.

In the beginning the hunting was good — mammoths, mastodons, Alaskan cave lions, huge ground sloths, plains grizzlies, camels and giant bison. The lakes, rivers and oceans teemed with fish. The native peoples developed a variety of small craft to use not only for hunting and fishing but also for general travel. A 1989 set of stamps shows the flat-bottomed hunting canoe of the Chipewyan Indians, the Haida craft carved from giant Pacific coast cedars and the Micmac vessel, which sometimes carried a sail — all contrasting with the slim, fast Inuit kayak.

1989 Chipewyan Canoe

1989 Inuit Kayak

1989 Haida Canoe

1989 Micmac Canoe

Although the hunters and fisherman ranged far afield, they also established villages and lived much like the early European settlers. Their customs and beliefs were different, however. Their gods were natural gods of wind, rain and fire. Environmental gods.

The native peoples believed that animals, fowl, fish and even trees and stones were endowed with immortal spirits and possessed supernatural powers to punish any who despised or

1953 Pacific Northwest Totem Pole

made waste of them. Reverently stylized representations of these spirits were often evoked in the objects the native peoples created for everyday use. They had no word for "art" in their languages.

The Indians of the Pacific Northwest carved elaborate poles to adorn their meeting places and dwellings. The stylized animals they shaped on cedar trees were heraldic symbols and crests, and each pole told a story of some real or legendary incident in the family's history. Some, like the one shown on a prized 1953 stamp, were 90 feet high.

1989 Frontlet

A ceremonial frontlet created by the Tsimshian people of the Northwest Coast Indians appears on a 1989 stamp. This magnificent frontlet, which was carved of wood and inlaid with stone and shell, was worn by a chief of the tribe at a traditional potlatch.

The natives lived off the land, killing what they needed to feed themselves, but they always killed with respect. They preserved the balance of nature because nature, despite her occasional tantrums, enabled them to survive.

The European arrivals brought an entirely different view of Canada's natural wealth and environment. Nature was not their god, so natural resources could be exploited without fear of divine reprisal. They wanted beaver skins, as many as could be trapped in the vast hinterland of Canada, to meet the voracious European demand for hats made from beaver pelts. Skilled Indian hunters obtained the skins, and the hats were made in France and Britain. One of several fur-trade stamps shows an Indian woman hanging a beaver pelt to dry near James Bay.

1955 Inuit

1968 Inuit Soapstone Carving

1968 Inuit Soapstone Carving

1977 Seal Hunter

1977 Inuit Hunter

1978 Inuit Woman Walking

Nature was particularly hard on the Inuit peoples, but they adapted over the millennia, developing a greater resistance to extreme cold than their Oriental forbearers. A 1955 stamp showing an Inuit in his kayak beside an iceberg conveys a sense of the awful loneliness of the High Arctic, a loneliness that is unrelieved by the presence of an airliner overhead.

Like the Indian nations, the Inuit developed their own forms of art. Inuit soapstone carving is at its best in the historic *Mother and Child* pieces presented to Princess Elizabeth in 1951, and illustrated on a pair of 1968 stamps. The popularity of Inuit carvings led to a rediscovery of their pictorial art, represented on stamps in hunting and fishing scenes, recreations of Inuit spirits and a brilliant print evoking the annual joy of the Return of the Sun. Other stamps show the building of summer tents and winter igloos, drumming and dancing.

A 1977 set of stamps shows, through prints and carvings, scenes of caribou, walrus and seal hunting and spear fishing. The following year a set showing Inuit travel methods was issued.

Other native peoples whose artifacts, dances and symbols have been honored on stamps are the Algonkian, the Iroquoian and the Subarctic Indians, who range from Labrador across to Alaska. The Plains Indians are recalled in the *Buffalo Chase*, a particularly fine stamp taken from an engraving by George Catlin. It shows a horseman racing after a magnificent animal.

Crowfoot, warrior chief of the Blackfoot, is commemorated on a 1986 stamp. He led his people in negotiating a treaty with Canada in 1877. The treaty Crowfoot negotiated and signed with James F. Macleod of the North West Mounted Police, and the depletion of the great herds of buffalo that once roamed the prairies, changed the way of life of the Plains Indians. They took up farming and ranching on the reservation lands provided them by the government. The great buffalo hunts of the 1870s, which had shaken the earth for miles around, were a thing of the past.

1973 Algonkian Couple

1972 Buffalo Chase

1978 Dogsled

1986 James F. Macleod

1974 Montagnais Naskapi Artifact

1986 Crowfoot, Blackfoot Chief

1975 Ojibwa Thunderbird

Chapter Eight

Transportation and Communication

The earliest explorers arrived on the shores of Canada by ship and continued their journeys inland by canoe. Water transportation has therefore been one of the central themes of Canadian history.

The canoe of today is regarded as a little sporting craft, but the fur traders of yesteryear paddled heavy birch-bark vessels 40-50 feet long and capable of carrying four tons of trading goods. The flat-bottomed York boat used by troops and merchants in the West and hefted over portages from Fort Erie to Vancouver was even larger.

Canadian shipbuilders included men who had never seen the sea because, before the Welland Canal provided a route around Niagara Falls and the Lachine Canal opened the way to the sea, ships on the Upper Lakes had to be built above the falls. In the 1880s the CPR Steamship Company built ocean-sized ships on the Clyde, cut them in two at Montréal and then spliced them together again on the shores of Lake Ontario. Canada's best-known wooden vessel is the racing schooner *Bluenose*, celebrated on two stamps. Other schooners illustrated on a stamp include a three-masted trader and a five-masted rum-runner from the Prohibition days. The oldest ship still in service in North America is the Muskoka Lakes steamer, *Segwun*. But the nation's most significant feat of shipbuilding is the HMS *St. Lawrence*, built at Kingston, Ontario, during the War of 1812. It was a three-decker battleship the size of Nelson's Victory and carrying more guns (112 to *Victory*'s 102). Singlehanded, and without firing a shot, the *St. Lawrence* ended the war on Lake Ontario; the smaller American warships took one look and scuttled for harbor.

1987 *Segwun*, a steamship built in 1887, still cruises Ontario's Muskoka Lakes

Amazingly, the great vessel was built in only six months. Its cast-iron fittings were shipped from England and laboriously hauled up the rapids from Montréal. After the war it was stripped of its masts and became part of a dock at Kingston, but it broke loose in a storm and sank.

1933 *Royal William*

The *Royal William*, launched at Québec in 1831, was a triumph of endurance and spirit rather than of shipbuilding. An ungainly side-wheeler of 182 feet in length, it was the first Canadian ship to cross the Atlantic by steam power. This famous passage of 1833 was recalled 100 years later on a stamp which shows the *Royal William* battling a heavy sea.

1988

1929

Canada's pride, the schooner **Bluenose**, is famous for its racing feats and also for the stamp issued (1929) in honor of one of its victories in the International Fisherman's Race. Many philatelists consider the stamp the most beautiful ever issued.

Built at Lunenberg, Nova Scotia as a combination fishing vessel and racing yacht, the **Bluenose** spent at least one season fishing off the Grand Banks of Newfoundland before her skipper, Captain Angus Walters, entered the schooner in the International Fishermen's Race off Halifax. **Bluenose** vanquished the challengers in 1921, 1922, 1923, 1931 and 1938. It sailed to the Chicago Fair of 1933 and crossed to England for the Silver Jubilee of George V.

When war came the schooner was tied up until a West Indian company bought it. Captain Walters had failed to raise money to keep it in Canada. The **Bluenose** worked as a Caribbean freighter until it was wrecked off Haiti in 1946.

The commemorative stamp shows the **Bluenose** beating the U.S. challenger **Columbia** in 1923. It is a composite picture, taken from photographs shot during the race and carefully arranged to conform to the pattern of the actual race.

Yet both *vessels shown are the Bluenose.* It couldn't lose.

The Royal William had been built as a coastal steamer but had become a financial liability; when its owners couldn't sell it locally, they decided to ship it across the Atlantic in hopes of finding a London buyer. So, on August 18, 1833, the steamer wheeled out of Pictou, Nova Scotia, with seven passengers, 324 tons of coal and a small cargo, including a collection of stuffed Canadian birds and a load of mail. It lost one engine in a gale and started to roll, but Captain John McDougall got it pumped out while he fixed the engine. Though he had to revert to sail power for a short period every four days while the salt was being cleaned out of the boilers, the *Royal William* made it to London in a record 25 days.

Samuel Cunard, a Halifax businessman who had originally lost money on the *Royal William*, was inspired to build bigger and better Atlantic paddle-steamers. He had the notion that they could be made to run on time like trains and therefore could carry the Royal Mail. He sailed to London and convinced the Admiralty that he could deliver the mail when no British shipowner could. Returning home with an exclusive contract, he built the RMS (Royal Mail Steamer) *Britannia*, the first vessel to hold that title and the first of the famous Cunard liners, ancestor of the *Queen Mary* and the *Queen Elizabeth*.

Britannia made its maiden voyage to Halifax in 1840 (soon followed by three sister ships). Charles Dickens, who sailed to Canada on the *Britannia* two years later, wrote a dismal account of the accommodations and food. But the mail got through.

While seafarers were plowing the oceans or ranging the plentiful fishing grounds, lake steamers carried passengers, freight and letters faster than the stagecoach.

But, beyond the routes of the lake steamers, travellers had to endure aching stagecoach journeys on dusty or muddy potholed roads — and that's where there were roads. In 1840 stagecoach driver William Weller drove from Toronto to Montreal in 35 hours and 40 minutes to win a $1000 bet.

1951 *North Star* Plane and Stagecoach

An imaginative 1951 stamp shows a four-engine plane flying over a mail coach, but it was the train that replaced the long-distance wagon in transcontinental mail delivery. The Iron Horse was welcomed wherever it arrived, although the sparks from its smokestack started fires and its wood-smoke blackened the skies. During the last century, smoke meant prosperity.

The first Iron Horse on the prairies was the *Countess of Dufferin*. It arrived in Winnipeg on October 9, 1877, floating on a barge because the westbound track of the CPR had not been completed.

1986 Locomotive

1984 *Countess of Dufferin*

The first Upper Canadian locomotive was manufactured in Toronto in 1853 and proudly named the *Toronto*. It had two driving wheels, a bulbous smokestack and a cowcatcher, which became a standard feature of North American engines. As trains grew longer, their engines got bigger, with up to eight great driving wheels.

Stamp series issued between 1983 and 1986 illustrates the growth of these steam-powered monsters, up to the time when they were replaced by the less impressive diesel engines.

1983 The *Toronto*

Train passengers barely noticed the first powered flight in Canada, made by 23-year-old John Alexander Douglas McCurdy

1983 *Silver Dart*, issued on the 50th anniversary of the first flight in Canada.

on February 23, 1909. He flew his flimsy *Silver Dart* half a mile across a frozen bay at Baddeck on Cape Breton — six years after the Wright brothers' historic flight. McCurdy was the first person in the British Empire to fly. He worked with Alexander Graham Bell at Bell's institute for the study of flight.

Flying caught on in Canada because, though then less comfortable than train travel, it was faster. Soon the country had more pilots per capita than any other nation. Many who had trained on the rickety biplanes of World War One came home to fly the bush planes that were replacing canoes as vehicles of exploration and transportation in the North.

1983 *Dorchester*

1985 Locomotive

1969 Alcock-Brown Flight

The first non-stop transatlantic flight — Alcock and Brown's 1919 run from Newfoundland to Ireland, in a twin-engine Vimy biplane — proved that airplanes could cover great distances, and Canada provided the distances to try their endurance. Alcock and Brown also carried the first transatlantic airmail; it bore Newfoundland stamps that were overprinted and surcharged $1.

1982 *Fairchild* FC-2W1

1982 *Norseman*

1982 *Fokker Super Universal*

1982 de Havilland *Beaver*

Bush planes celebrated on stamps include the Curtiss JN-4 *Canuck*, which flew the first airmail between Montreal and Toronto; the *Fairchild* FC-2W1, which dropped mail bags by parachute on Sept-Iles, Quebec; the *Norseman*, first true bush plane, and the *Fokker Super Universal*, both produced by Robert Noorduyn of Montreal; and the long-serving de Havilland *Beaver*. The *Beaver* proved so reliable that used ones still sell for more than their original price.

1928 Airmail

1930 Airmail Mercury

Airmail service began officially in 1928. The first special airmail stamps portrayed two angels hovering over a globe. On another stamp, Mercury, the messenger of the gods, was recruited to represent amazing speeds of more than 100 miles per hour. The final airmail stamp, issued in 1946, abandoned gods and airplanes and showed a Canada goose in flight.

A major Canadian contribution to the Allied war effort in World War Two was the British Commonwealth Air Training Plan, which trained 130,000 raw recruits from Britain, the dominions and other Allied nations. Fifty-five percent of these served in the RCAF, which grew from a squadron of fighter planes, flying Canadian-built Hawker *Hurricanes* in the Battle of Britain, to 28 squadrons, plus a bomber group which, at the end of the war, had put a quarter of a million Canadians in uniform.

After the war the first Canadian-designed jet fighter, the CF-100, became the first straight-winged combat aircraft to break the sound barrier. The Avro *Jetliner*, 1949, was the first jet transport in North America. De Havilland Canada added the *Dash 7*, the short-take-off-and-landing airliner.

1942-43 Airmail, depicting pilots from the British Commonwealth Air Training Plan.

1980 Avro Canada CF-100   1980 Hawker Hurricane   1981 Avro C-102   1981 de Havilland *Dash-7*

1963

Sir Casimir Stanislaus Gzowski was the most romantic of railway builders. Born into the landed gentry of Poland, he fought the Russians as an army officer then was captured and exiled to the United States. There he became first a lawyer then a civil engineer, while teaching fencing and music.

He moved to Canada in 1842 and built roads, bridges, lighthouses and harbors before becoming a railway promoter. His construction firm built the Grand Trunk Railway, which was later named the Canadian National.

The Gzowski Medal is the oldest prize awarded by the Canadian Society of Civil Engineers.

When the St. Lawrence Seaway was opened by Queen Elizabeth and President Dwight D. Eisenhower in 1959 — a historic event commemorated by the postal service — Canada's transportation pattern was set. Saltwater ships could now sail from the Atlantic to the far tip of Lake Superior, jets whizzed overhead and trains still ran on time.

Much remained to be done on land, on water and in the air, but already Canadians were looking up far up and out — into space. In 1962 the first Canadian-made satellite, *Alouette I*, was launched from California by a U.S. rocket and settled into orbit over the equator. Three years later *Alouette II* was launched, and the

1959 Seaway

1966 *Alouette II*

1947 Alexander Graham Bell

1974 Invention of the Telephone

event was commemorated the following year on a stamp. These were the latest, but by no means the first, in Canadian communications initiatives.

In 1877 the Reverend Thomas Henderson, acting as Alexander Graham Bell's Canadian agent, received his first shipment of telephones — eight wooden hand-held machines and eight box ones — and reported: "The telephone is exciting some interest and I have no doubt will become popular in Canada."

Some three years earlier Bell had invented the device, a by-product of his work with the deaf. To settle the argument over its birthplace, he declared that he devised it in Brantford, Ontario, and later tested it in Boston. He made the first "long-distance" call between Brantford and nearby Paris, Ontario, reading Hamlet's "To be or not to be" soliloquy — the first Shakespeare by wire.

Mr. Henderson was right about the telephone's popularity. Canadians once held the record for making more telephone calls than any other nationality.

1974

He did not go over the falls in a barrel, but William Hamilton Merritt, an entrepreneur from St. Catharines, Ontario, conquered Niagara. He bypassed the falls by canal and then bridged the great gorge. His 1974 stamp marks the 150th anniversary of the start of construction of his Welland Canal, which lifted ships between Lake Ontario and Lake Erie through a series of locks and opened up the Great Lakes waterway. Now deepened and widened, it is still a vital part of today's seaway system.

Not content with this, Merritt undertook to build a railway bridge across the Niagara Gorge — the first suspension bridge in the world to carry the weight of a train. First, his engineers had to get a cable across the fierce river and up the cliff on the other side. In 1847 they held a kite-flying contest and offered a prize of $10 to the owner of the first kite to cross the river. An American boy won the prize when his kite snagged a tree on the Canadian side. Its string was then used to pull a light rope across, which, in turn, then pulled across a heavy rope attached to a cable, and the first bridge arose.

Merritt has been described as a Father of Canadian Transportation.

Guglielmo Marconi chose Signal Hill in St. John's, Newfoundland, to erect the 200-foot masts and fly the kite that would receive the first transatlantic wireless message. The Italian-born inventor, whose portrait appears on a 1974 stamp, was waiting on Signal Hill one December night in 1901 when he heard three faint peeps — the Morse letter "S" — come in over 2,100 miles of ether from Cornwall, England.

1974 Marconi

A lesser-known inventor, Reginald Aubrey Fessenden, born in Bolton, Quebec, used a different theory of sound-waves and devised a communications medium which probably had an even greater impact — AM radio. A year before Marconi's transatlantic triumph, Fessenden had transmitted his own voice by wireless over a distance of one mile. On Christmas Eve, 1906, he made the first full-blown radio broadcast — to radio operators aboard ships off the Massachusetts coast. He announced his own program, sang a carol, played his violin and cranked out Handel's *Largo* on his phonograph, becoming the world's first disk jockey. Fessenden followed this with 500 other inventions, including an aircraft altimeter.

1987 Reginald Aubrey Fessenden, inventor

Other Canadian communications breakthroughs celebrated on stamps include laying of the earliest undersea cable in North America, from New Brunswick to Prince Edward Island, by Frederick Newton Gisborne (1852) and the first photograph published by half-tone engraving (Georges-Edouard Desbarats and William Leggo, 1869).

1987 G.E. Desbarats and W. Leggo

1987 Undersea Cable

Chapter Nine

Industry and War

In colonial days, manufacturing in Canada was discouraged and at times forbidden by both France and Britain. As the colonial masters saw it, Canada's purpose was to export raw materials and import finished goods. After Confederation, Sir John A. Macdonald brought in his National Policy which, shorn of its flag-waving rhetoric, meant high tariffs against imports. It encouraged new industry, but Canadians would be regarded as "hewers of wood and drawers of water" for a long time. Agriculture, forestry, and mining were the main industries of the new nation, and this aspect of the Canadian tradition is portrayed extensively on stamps.

To begin with, the settlers hewed and drew for themselves; they were mainly subsistence farmers intent on feeding their families. They sowed seed by hand and harvested the crops with sickles or scythes, threshing it with flails. The cultivation of large crops was impossible. The revolution in farming began in the 1850s with the introduction of the mechanical reaper. Daniel Massey produced reapers at the farm-machinery factory he founded in Ontario in 1847. His firm, which became Massey-Harris and later Massey-Ferguson, was an early giant of Canadian industry. Labor-saving machines such as Massey's reaper made possible the tremendous expansion of agriculture across Canada, and seemingly endless acres of waving wheat became one of the most poignant images of this nation.

1930 Harvesting Wheat

1946 Combine

The tractor, first powered by steam then by gasoline and diesel, replaced the once-prized horses that did the heavy work on the farm. In 1922 a tractor was incorporated in a combined harvester-thresher, a machine which had such an impact on Canadian agriculture that it earned two separate stamps, one issued in 1930 and the other in 1946.

Although coal had been mined in Cape Breton since 1720, logging succeeded the fur trade as the major export industry of Eastern Canada. Logs were delivered from the inland forests to the shores of Nova Scotia, New Brunswick and Quebec, where Canada's early shipbuilding centres were located. It took 4,000 trees to

1958 Miner Panning for Gold

1978 Athabasca Tar Sands

1950 Oil Wells

1914-18 War Tax Stamp

1938 Memorial Chamber, Ottawa

make one wooden battleship so, by the end of the nineteenth century, most of the good trees in Eastern Canada were gone. The lumberjacks moved on. Many went to British Columbia to pan for gold.

A stamp issued on its centennial recalls the 1858 Cariboo Gold Rush. Hordes of men arrived in B.C., mostly via the American West Coast. Some stayed behind to settle and open up vast areas of the future province of British Columbia. Then came the Klondike strike of 1896. More men and women flooded into northern B.C. to climb the impossible Chilkoot Pass to try their luck in Bonanza Creek. Only a few found their gold in the river beds, but many made fortunes catering to the miners in the flophouses and barrooms of Dawson City.

Black, sticky crude oil is far less appealing than the magic metal, but vast underground lakes of it turned out to be far more valuable than pokes of gold dust and nuggets. The explorer and trader Peter Pond had noted black seepages along the Athabasca River as early as 1778, but nobody paid attention at the time. Pond, a dubious character who had been tried and acquitted of murdering another trader, had discovered the Athabasca Tar Sands, the great wealth of which is symbolized in a stamp issued 200 years after Pond's discovery.

The single most dramatic scene in Canada's petroleum industry is the blowing in of the first gusher at Leduc, Alberta, in 1947, an event which was illustrated on a stamp. It was the 134th drilled by Vernon "Dry Hole" Hunter and, when it came in, it sent "a beautiful ring of black smoke floating skyward." Alberta's oil boom was on.

1978 Cobalt Silver Mine **1983 Nickel Discovery**

Most of the rich minerals of Northern Ontario seem to have been discovered by accident. Blacksmith Fred LaRose threw his hammer at a passing fox, missed and hit a rock, uncovering the wondrous vein of silver in Cobalt, Ontario. Another blacksmith, Tom Flanagan, struck copper while blasting a cutting for the CPR near Sudbury. The copper was heavily laced with nickel, at the time considered a nuisance metal. Later it became more valuable than copper, and Tom had located the richest nickel deposit in the world, as the stamp commemorating the discovery revealed. Then, at Timmins, Harry Preston accidentally stuck his boot through a lump of moss and revealed the rock face of the Dome, first of the great Porcupine gold mines.

The two world wars increased and diversified Canada's industrial capacity. In addition to munitions, vehicles and various pieces of equipment never before manufactured in Canada were produced in staggering quantities.

The only special stamps put out during the Great War (1914-18) were war tax issues, indicating that an extra one cent had been added to the price to help pay for the war effort.

A stamp commemorating a century of peace between the United States and Canada was ready to go in 1914, but it was never issued because it seemed inappropriate to put out a peace stamp when the biggest war in history was raging.

During the Great War, 42,042 Canadians died. They are remembered in a 1938 stamp showing the Memorial Chamber in the Peace Tower in Ottawa and its Altar of Remembrance, with books listing those who fell during Ypres, Vimy Ridge and many other battles. (New books were later added listing the names of the dead of World War Two and the Korean conflict.) A 1939 stamp shows the Ottawa war memorial that was unveiled by King George VI.

1939 Ottawa National War Memorial

Canadian airmen distinguished themselves in the Royal Flying Corps (later the Royal Air Force) in World War One. They included ace pilot William Avery (Billy) Bishop, who shot down 82 enemy aircraft, and Roy Brown, who downed German ace Baron Manfred von Richthofen. Canadian pilots wore long leather coats and breeches in their open cockpits. World War Two pilots wore similar helmets and goggles with one-piece flying suits and a parachute harness. Today's jet pilots wear elaborate space-age gear.

1984 stamp commemorates the 60th anniversary of the permanent establishment of the RCAF.

Stamps issued between 1939 and 1945 showed what Canadians at home were doing for the war effort. They depict the destroyers, corvettes, field guns and tanks built in Canada for the battle of the Atlantic and the invasion of Europe. Also — for this was equally important — one shows a grain elevator, symbol of the food Canadians were sending to sustain the hungry British.

1942 Grain Elevator

Perhaps the most touching of the war stamps is the 1968 portrait of Dr. John McCrae, poet and soldier, who wrote "In Flanders Fields, the poppies grow, between the crosses, row on row...". A medical officer with the First Canadian Contingent, he composed the famous poem in 20 minutes while mourning the death of a friend in the second battle of Ypres. McCrae died of pneumonia in 1918 and is buried in France beneath one of those crosses. But a light still burns continuously in his honor in a garden beside the house in Guelph, Ontario, where he was born.

1968 50th anniversary issue of the death of John McCrae.

Chapter Ten

Sporting Stamps

Canada's first team sport was lacrosse, invented and played by Indians long before recorded history began. They called it *baggataway*. French pioneers thought the stick used in the game, with its triangular head and rawhide-strip pocket, looked like a bishop's crozier or hook, so they named the game *la crosse*, a heritage that is depicted in a 1968 stamp.

The object of lacrosse is to carry or pass the ball in one's stick while fighting off opponents who are wielding their sticks. It was, and still is, a tough game. The rules were first set down in the 1860s by Montréal dentist Dr. George W. Beers.

In winter lacrosse was played on skates, which may have given some British immigrants the idea of adapting their game of field hockey to what would become Canada's most popular national sport. The first hockey game is said to have been held on the frozen harbor of Kingston, Ontario, about the time Dr. Beers was setting down the rules for lacrosse. The players probably tried using a ball at first, for the word "puck," meaning something you poke at, came later.

In the 1956 stamp commemorating hockey, the player moving the puck up the ice wears a sweater bearing the name "Canada."

1968 Lacrosse

1986 Ice Hockey

1956 Hockey Players

Basketball was invented in 1891 by Canadian James A. Naismith from Almonte, Ontario, but not in Canada. He was teaching physical education in Springfield, Massachusetts, when he tried to combine various features of soccer, American football and field hockey and ended up with a game quite unlike any of

1976 Basketball, a game invented by a Canadian.

1988 Baseball

1980 Ned Hanlan

1982 Royal Canadian Henley Regatta

1969 Curling

1987 Cross-Country Skiing

them. He decreed that there should be nine players per team simply because he had 18 students in his class that year.

Baseball, the great American game, was probably developed from the English sport of rounders. Abner Doubleday is credited with creating the sport of baseball in Cooperstown, New York, in 1839. But the first recorded game was played a year earlier — at Beachville in southwestern Ontario. The date was June 4, 1838, and the teams, representing Oxford County and Zorra Township, played with cedar bats. This fact was so little known that, in 1988, a stamp was issued to mark the 150th year of the sport in Canada.

Tom Longboat, who became the long-distance champion of North America, was the greatest Canadian runner of his time. Longboat, an Indian, was described as "the swiftest of his race since Deerfoot." He was born on the Six Nations Reserve near Brantford, Ontario, in 1887, and his Iroquois name was *Cog-Wa-Gee*. He won the Hamilton "Around the Bay" race in 1906, despite odds of a hundred to one against him, then the 15-mile Toronto Marathon for three consecutive years. He once raced a horse for 12 miles and won.

When war broke out he ran 60 miles to enlist in the 180th Sportsmen's Battalion. As a soldier, he was described as "the most difficult recruit to train in the whole British Empire" — surely another record. Nobody, including his sergeant-major, could handle Tom Longboat because nobody could catch up with him.

Ned Hanlan (or Hanlon) was Tom's equal, but on water. He was the best oarsman in the world and won the world single-sculls championship six times between 1879-84. He lived on Toronto Island, at Hanlan's (or Hanlon's) Point — nobody could ever get his name right — when one had to row a boat to get to the mainland in summer. During these crossings he developed the muscles and style that brought him victory.

The century-old Royal Canadian Henley Regatta was recognized as a world-class rowing event in 1982, but Canadian team oarsmen had made their mark long before that. At the 1912 Olympics in Sweden, the eight Toronto oarsmen received a special medal — for losing. They were beaten by inches after a tremendous duel with the English boat. After the race it was discovered that the course gave the English a boat-length or more advantage. Asked if he wished to appeal, the Canadian coach gallantly replied that the Englishmen had rowed well and won. "Such mishaps are not to be cried about by sportsmen," he declared. His sportsmanship so impressed the king of Sweden that he ordered a special medal to be struck for the Torontonians.

Curling, "the roaring game," came from Scotland, where it had been played with large stones worn smooth in river beds. Teams assisted or retarded their passage along the ice with long-handled scrubbing brushes. Canadians used corn whisk-brooms.

The father of Canadian cross-country skiing is Herman "Jack Rabbit" Smith-Johannsen, a Norwegian-born engineer who laid ski trails in the Laurentians, north of Montréal, and generally opened up a vast area to skiers. He was coach of the 1932 Canadian Olympic ski team, created the Canadian Ski Marathon and advised on trails for the 1980 Winter Olympics.

As host to the Montréal Olympics in 1976, the Calgary Winter Olympics in 1988, and various Commonwealth and Pan-American games, Canadians have seen and taken part in the best of amateur competitive sport. Figure-skating, swimming, rowing and sailing, track and field, as well as the combat sports of fencing, boxing and judo are represented on stamps. The beauty of motion is demonstrated in the sculptures *The Sprinter* and *The Plunger*, by Robert Tait McKenzie. These were represented on stamps in 1975.

1975 *The Plunger*

1975 *The Sprinter*

1976 Olympic Torch

International events are often commemorated on stamps, because the stamps make popular souvenirs. Between the big events, Canadians continue to enjoy the quieter pastimes of fishing, hunting, cycling, jogging or simply walking.

1976 Olympic Medal Ceremony

All forms of exercise took on new meaning in 1980 when 22-year-old Terry Fox hopped and skipped 5,373 kilometres on an artificial leg. He had lost his leg to cancer and began his Marathon of Hope run from St. John's to Victoria to prove that cancer could be beaten. He lost. At Thunder Bay his cancer caught up with him again and took him off his long, long road. But his effort not only raised $23 million for cancer research, it also gave hope to those stricken by the disease and inspired thousands of physically disabled to take part in athletics.

1976 Archer in Wheelchair, Olympiad for the Physically Disabled, Toronto.

Terry's feat was so remarkable that he was one of the very few Canadians to be remembered on a stamp so soon after his death.

Terry died but other disabled Canadians picked up the torch. Steve Fonyo, a one-legged man, ran 7,924 kilometres across Canada, and Rick Hansen went around the world in a wheelchair. Sport in Canada takes many forms, but none more significant than such dramatic victories of mind and spirit over body.

1982 Terry Fox Marathon of Hope Issue. Terry died before he could complete his task.